FIFTY POEMS OF ʿAṬṬĀR

Kenneth Avery is a graduate of Sydney and Melbourne Universities, and a specialist in Sufi and Persian literature. His Ph.D. thesis was published in 2004 as: *A Psychology of Early Sufi samāʿ: Listening and Altered States* (RoutledgeCurzon). He is a writer and teacher, and lives in rural Victoria, Australia.

Ali Alizadeh holds a Ph.D. in Professional Writing from Deakin University, Melbourne, and teaches writing and literature at universities in Australia and Asia. His books of poetry include *Eyes in Times of War* and *eliXir: a story in poetry*. His translations of Persian poetry have been widely published.

Anomaly

An anomaly deviates from a norm, is difficult to recognize or classify. *Anomaly* is a series which publishes heterodox, eccentric and heretical works. Mashing fact with fiction, poetry with philosophy, fish with fowl, *Anomaly* is a laboratory of unprecedented writings.

a re.press series

FIFTY POEMS OF ʿAṬṬĀR

Texts, translations and analysis by

Kenneth Avery and Ali Alizadeh

re.press Melbourne 2007

re.press

PO Box 75, Seddon, 3011, Melbourne, Australia

http://www.re-press.org

First published 2007

British Library Cataloguing-in-Publication Data
A catalogue record for this book is available from the British Library

Library of Congress Cataloguing-in-Publication Data
A catalogue record for this book is available from the Library of Congress

National Library of Australia Cataloguing-in-Publication Data

Farīd al-Dīn ʿAṭṭār, d. ca. 1230.
[Poems. Selections]
Fifty poems of ʿAṭṭār :.

Bibliography.
ISBN 9780980305210 (pbk.).

1. ʿAṭṭār , Farīd al-Dīn , d. ca. 1230 - Translations into English. 2. Sufi poetry, Persian - Translations into English. I. Avery, Kenneth. II. Alizadeh, Ali. III. Title. (Series : Anomaly).

891.5511

Designed and Typeset by *A&R*
Typeset in *Garamond*

Printed on-demand in Australia, the United Kingdom and the United States
This book is produced sustainably using plantation timber, and printed in the destination market on demand reducing wastage and excess transport

TABLE OF CONTENTS

ACKNOWLEDGEMENTS

Thank you to the publishers of *ʿAṭṭār's Dīwān* in Tehran, Sharka Intishārāt ʿIlmī u Farhangī. Earlier versions of the translations of ghazals 1 and 31 have been published in Ali Alizadeh, *Eyes in Times of War*, Cambridge, Salt Publishing, 2006.

INTRODUCTION

'Shaykh Farīd al-Dīn Muḥammad 'Aṭṭār of Nishapur is one of the greatest and most celebrated Persian poets and literary figures'.[1] So the Iranian scholar Taqī Tafaḍḍulī introduces the poet in the preface to his edition of 'Aṭṭār's lyrics. In the West, 'Aṭṭār is similarly regarded as an important figure in classical Persian literature and among the most famous Sufi authors of the medieval period. He is, however, probably less well known than his illustrious successors among Sufi poets, notably Rūmī and Ḥāfiẓ, his reputation suffering from an overshadowing effect. Yet 'Aṭṭār is one of the canonical masters of Sufi poetry who has had an immense impact on later writers. As a creative, sophisticated and challenging early mystical poet, his work deserves wider recognition and more serious attention.

'Aṭṭār is best known in the West for his *Manṭiq al-ṭayr* (*Conference of the Birds*). This work in rhymed couplet or *mathnawī* form tells the charming allegory of a group of birds who search for their mythical 'king', named the *sī-murgh*, only to find that there are thirty birds (*sī murgh*) who complete this journey of self discovery. His other works in *mathnawī* form are much less known; they all deal by allegorical means, or in more direct didactic form, with aspects of the Sufi path to divine knowledge. The most important of these other *mathnawī*s are the *Ilāhī-nāma* (*Book of God*), about a king who tries to inspire his six sons with non-worldly aims; the *Muṣībat-nāma* (*Book of Affliction*), concerning a Sufi's allegorical journey of self-knowledge; and the *Asrār-nāma* (*Book of Mysteries*), a more direct didactic work.[2] His single extant prose writing

1. Farīd al-Dīn 'Aṭṭār, *Dīwān*, Taqī Tafaḍḍulī (ed.), Tehran, Bungāh-i Tarjama u Nashri Kitāb, 1967, p. 25.

2. For a thorough analysis of these works, see Hellmut Ritter, *Das Meer der Seele: Mensch, Welt und Gott in den Geschichten des Farīduddīn 'Aṭṭār*, Leiden, E.J. Brill, 1978.

is a hagiography of the early Sufi masters, the *Tadhkirat al-awliyāʾ* (*Memorial of the Saints*). This is a work for a popular audience, containing much information on the Sufi masters and 'friends' of God written in a lively and entertaining form. There are numerous other works of doubtful authenticity attributed to ʿAṭṭār,[3] but by any criterion, he was a prolific, creative and original author.

His collection of lyric poetry or *Dīwān* contains a large number of *ghazals*. These are short lyric poems with rhyming couplets of the form aa ba ca da ......; the poet's name occurs in the end couplet; and generally speaking, love is the subject matter. There are also thirty or so *qaṣīdas* in the collection, these being much longer lyrics of the same rhyme scheme. It may be claimed that ʿAṭṭār established the use of the *ghazal* form as the principal vehicle for Sufi love poetry, though Sanāʾī of Ghazna (d. 1131) pioneered its use among mystical poets. ʿAṭṭār's lyrics are concerned with the theme of divine love in its multifarious aspects, of the incomparable beauty of the Beloved, the hopes and aspirations of the lover, and his anguish at not reaching Her presence. The essence of ʿAṭṭār's faith and worldview is his acceptance of the all-pervasive reality of God, the infinite and all-encompassing Being who is the ground of the universe and of the human soul. The soul's realization of its oneness with God is the aim of human life and the goal of the mystical quest; all else is nought and valueless. ʿAṭṭār's poems are imbued with the inspiration and spirit of genuine mystical faith, in the words of Jan Rypka, 'marked by transports of ecstatic fervour', 'distinguished by a great emphasis on mystical symbolism and by infectious enthusiasm'.[4] Heshmat Moayyad writes: 'The search for divine truth is the leitmotif of his entire corpus, and the realization that it lies beyond reach is the source of his anguish'.[5] ʿAṭṭār's poetry is always inspiring and full of freshness and vitality, containing many original and graceful expressions of the Sufi lover's divine quest.

The aim of the present work is to offer a study of ʿAṭṭār's *ghazals*; his poetry has for too long been neglected in the Western world, and a presentation and analysis of his work is overdue. The book attempts to deal with the problems of interpretation and general approach to his poetry, to examine the imagery and themes, and try to understand

---

3. See Hellmut Ritter, "Aṭṭār', in *Encyclopaedia of Islam*, vol. I, new ed., Leiden, E.J. Brill, 1960-, pp. 752-5.

4. J. Rypka, 'Poets and Prose Writers of the Late Saljuq and Mongol Periods', in *The Cambridge History of Iran*, J.A. Boyle (ed.), vol. 5, Cambridge, Cambridge University Press, 1968, p. 590.

5. Heshmat Moayyad, 'Lyric Poetry', in E. Yarshater (ed.), *Persian Literature*, Albany (N.Y.), Persian Heritage Foundation, 1988, p. 136.

the mystical sense and spirit of these poems. This book also provides a lengthy section of texts and translations from fifty poems chosen from the *Dīwān*.

ʿAṬṬĀR'S LIFE AND TIME

Unfortunately there are few reliable details on the biography of ʿAṭṭār, and much disagreement about even the basic dates of his birth and death. The latter has been placed at widely differing times, as early as 1190, according to the inscription on his tomb which was, however, erected much later. According to some sources, his death occurred as late as 1230. It is more likely that he was killed, along with most of the population of his native city, Nishapur, by the conquering Mongols in 1220-1.[6]

We know for certain that he lived most of his life in his native city, and there is no real evidence of his having travelled extensively. ʿAṭṭār's writings say little about his life or the times in which he lived. This is not surprising since they are all works of a religious nature, dealing with spiritual subjects, and having little occasion for topical or biographical references. He does say, however, that he was a pharmacist/physician with a shopfront in Nishapur, and that he had many patients to care for. In the *Khusraw-nāma* (*Book of King Khusraw*) he mentions that he wrote two of his books while attending to five hundred patients daily.[7] His name, ʿAṭṭār, means literally a perfumer or apothecary, and it seems that he inherited the business from his father. Having an assured livelihood meant that he could spurn the art of being a professional poet, particularly that of a court eulogist or panegyric poet[8]. Such writers had to depend on the whims of princes, and were forced to write poetry to order, often to flatter or cajole their patrons. Apart from financial needs, however, ʿAṭṭār had a deep personal distaste for what he saw as demeaning and mercenary poetic arts which were completely opposed to the otherworldly values of the Sufi life.[9]

6. See, Benedickt Reinert, "ʿAṭṭār', in *Encyclopaedia Iranica*, E. Yarshater (ed.), vol. III, London, New York, Routledge & Kegan Paul, 1989, p. 21; Badīʿ Furūzānfar, *Sharḥ-i aḥwāl wa naqd wa taḥlīl-i āthār-i Shaykh Farīd al-Dīn Muḥammad ʿAṭṭār*, Tehran, Kitābfurūshī Dih-khudā, 1353 a.h.s, p. 91; ʿAṭṭār, *Dīwān*, Taqī Tafaḍḍulī (ed.), Tehran, Bungāh-i Tarjama u Nashri Kitāb, 1967, p. 26; and Hellmut Ritter, 'ʿAṭṭār', in *Encyclopaedia of Islam*, vol. I, new ed., Leiden, E.J. Brill, 1960-, p. 752.

7. J.A. Boyle *The Ilāhīnama or Book of God of Farīd al-Dīn ʿAṭṭār*, Manchester, Manchester University Press, 1976, p.xx; and ʿAṭṭār, *Dīwān*, Taqī Tafaḍḍulī (ed.), Tehran, Bungāh-i Tarjama u Nashri Kitāb, 1967, p. 27.

8. So Tafaḍḍulī, in ʿAṭṭār, *Dīwān*, p. 28.

9. See further, Hellmut Ritter, *Das Meer der Seele: Mensch, Welt und Gott in den Geschichten*

The 15th century biographer of Persian poets, Dawlatshāh Samarqandī (d. after 1487) records that 'Aṭṭār spent most of his life in Shādyākh, a suburb of Nishapur where his pharmacy was located. Both Dawlatshāh and his contemporary 'Abd al-Raḥmān Jāmī (d. 1492), an important biographer and Sufi author himself, relate a story about 'Aṭṭār's 'repentance' and conversion to the religious life. A wandering dervish abruptly came to the shop one day and questioned 'Aṭṭār on his preparedness for departure from this world. The dervish suddenly died in 'Aṭṭār's presence, which troubled him so much that he immediately abandoned his shop and retired for some years to the Sufi lodge of a certain Rukn al-Dīn Akkāf.[10] Dawlatshāh and Jāmī also relate a story about 'Aṭṭār giving a copy of his *Asrār-nāma* to the young Jalāl al-Dīn Rūmī, whose family was travelling through Nishapur after fleeing from Balkh in about 1215. 'Aṭṭār on this occasion prophesied to Jalāl al-Dīn's father about the future eminence of his son.[11] These accounts may be more than pious traditions, as such legends often contain some kernel of truth.

As for education, his writings show that he was well versed in many of the traditional areas of learning current in his day. This includes the religious curriculum of Qur'ānic studies, *ḥadīth* (sacred Traditions) and law. As well, he displays knowledge of literature, philosophy, astronomy and other sciences, including the medical and pharmaceutical studies associated with his occupation.[12] We have little information about the teachers or the Sufi masters whom 'Aṭṭār would have known. Hellmut Ritter, who has written an extensive work on the *mathnawī*s, even goes so far as to claim that he was not actually a Sufi.[13] This is based on 'Aṭṭār's statement in the introduction to the *Tadhkirat al-awliyā'*[14] that although he is not one of the Sufis, he made himself 'similar' to them, quoting an Arabic proverb or tradition that 'one who is similar to a group

---

des Farīduddīn 'Aṭṭār, Leiden, E.J. Brill, 1978, p. 156.

10. Dawlatshāh Samarqandī, *Tadhkirat al-shu'arā'*, M. Ramḍānī (ed.), Tehran, Khāwar, 1344 a.h.s., pp. 140-1; 'Abd al-Raḥman b. Aḥmad Jāmī, *Nafaḥāt al-uns min ḥaḍarāt al-quds*, M. Tawḥīdī Pūr (ed.), Tehran, 'Ilmī, 1375 a.h.s., p. 599.

11. Dawlatshāh Samarqandī, *Tadhkirat al-shu'arā'*, M. Ramḍānī (ed.), Tehran, Khāwar, 1344 a.h.s., p. 145; 'Abd al-Raḥman b. Aḥmad Jāmī, *Nafaḥāt al-uns min ḥaḍarāt al-quds*, M. Tawḥīdī Pūr (ed.), Tehran, 'Ilmī, 1375 a.h.s., p. 599.

12. Pūrān Shajī'ī, *Jihān-bīnī-yi 'Aṭṭār*, Tehran, Ḥaydarī, 1373 a.h.s., pp. 17-8.

13. Hellmut Ritter, "Aṭṭār', in *Encyclopaedia of Islam*, vol. I, new ed., Leiden, E.J. Brill, 1960-, p. 752; and Hellmut Ritter, *Das Meer der Seele: Mensch, Welt und Gott in den Geschichten des Farīduddīn 'Aṭṭār*, Leiden, E.J. Brill, 1978, p. 152.

14. 'Aṭṭār, Farīd al-Dīn, *The Tadhkiratu 'l-awliyā*, R.A. Nicholson (ed.), 2 vols., vol. 1, London & Leiden, E.J. Brill; Luzac & Co, 1905-7, p. 4.

of people is one of them'. This disclaimer occurs in the context of ʿAṭṭār giving his reasons for writing his hagiography of the early Sufi masters. It is thus likely that he mentions his own position as an act of modesty and deference, indicating his high regard for the early masters and not presuming to claim a place among them. In a way, this accords with the Nishapurian *malāmatī* attitude of concealing one's private views.[15] In any case, the author shows an intimate personal knowledge of the Sufi path, and it is difficult to believe that his writings are the work of a merely sympathetic outsider. Apart from the sincerity and genuineness of his experience evidenced in his writings, ʿAṭṭār is constantly urging his readers to abandon the world, travel the Sufi path, and attain to divine unitary experience. Could he have urged this time and again if he was hypocritically not a traveller on the path himself?

As a Sufi writer, ʿAṭṭār stands among a long line of famous scholars and mystics who originated from the province of Khurāsān in north-east Iran. Three names worthy of mention are ʿAbd al-Raḥman al-Sulamī (d. 1021), an important Sufi biographer and Traditionist; Abū ʿl-Qāsim al-Qushayrī (d. 1072), the author of the famous *Risāla* (*Treatise*); and Abū Ḥāmid al-Ghazālī (d. 1111), the celebrated theologian whose famous *Iḥyāʾ ʿulūm al-dīn* (*Revival of the Religious Sciences*) attempted a synthesis of Sunnī Islam with a moderate form of Sufi thought. Ghazālī taught for a time at the famous Niẓāmīya *madrasa* in Nishapur, which had only recently been established there. All of these figures had some links with Nishapur, which in the 11th and 12th centuries had developed into an important cultural and spiritual centre of the Eastern Islamic world.

During these centuries Nishapur was a flourishing and prosperous city, an important centre of economic activity, including the production of textiles and luxury clothing, as well as various arts and crafts, most notably ceramics, from sun-dried bricks to the highest quality pottery. Geographically and economically, Nishapur was favourably located on the great East-West trade route, at the junction of the overland route to Afghanistan and India, and the main east-west highway between the Levant and Central Asia.[16] The city's prosperity was reflected in an ascendant merchant and artisan class, and influential groups of scholars and religious figures from the two rival *madhhab*s or legal schools of

15. See J. Spencer Trimingham, *The Sufi Orders in Islam*, Oxford, Clarendon Press, 1971, pp. 265-6.

16. Richard W. Bulliet, *The Patricians of Nishapur: A Study in Medieval Islamic Social History*, Cambridge (Mass.), Harvard University Press, 1972, pp. 5,12.

Khurāsān, the Ḥanafīs and Shāfiʿīs. Among the ordinary people these religious orientations contended with the ascetic and pietistic Karrāmīya sect for popular support.[17]

In Nishapur during the 10th and 11th centuries, the Sufi way became closely linked with the institutions and practices of mainstream Islam within the city.[18] With the decline of the Abbasid Empire, local regimes replaced the central authority, and the rule of the invading Ghaznavid and later the Seljuq dynasties meant that independent religious elites were important in helping to govern, as well as providing the regime with social and religious legitimacy. The scholar-jurists (*'ulamā'*) and the Sufi groups developed their own forms of organization and structures independently from the state. These came to represent Islam socially and doctrinally, and these religious organizations in turn received state support by way of the building of *madrasa*s (schools) and *khānaqāh*s (Sufi lodges), the payment of salaries, and other endowments.[19]

In Nishapur during the century prior to the time of 'Aṭṭār, the Sufi way gained the ascendancy in mysticism and piety. Other forms of mysticism such as the *malāmatīya* (those seeking to bring blame on themselves) had been popular earlier; Sulamī, for example, came from a family where this form of piety was dominant. The Sufis of Nishapur were also predominantly of the Shāfiʿī *madhhab,* and both Sufi teaching and mainstream theology sat comfortably with each other in the institutions and religious life of the city.

The three Sufi scholars mentioned above, Sulamī, Qushayrī and Ghazālī, among many others, were part of a Khurāsānian movement of defining and defending the legitimacy of Sufi thought and practice against detractors and opponents.[20]

The 11th century also saw the development of Sufi *khānaqāh*s (lodges or retreats) in Khurāsān, an important development in the formation and organization of Sufi brotherhoods and orders. Prior to this, the practice of Sufis had been limited to small circles of disciples around a master, meeting in private homes or mosques. The new *khānaqāh*s became

17. E. Honigmann (& C.E. Bosworth), 'Nīshāpūr', in *Encyclopaedia of Islam*, vol. VIII, Leiden, E.J. Brill, 1960-, p. 63.

18. Margaret Malamud, 'Sufi Organizations and Structures of Authority in Medieval Nishapur', *International Journal of Middle East Studies,* no. 26, 1994, p. 427.

19. Margaret Malamud, 'Sufi Organizations and Structures of Authority in Medieval Nishapur', p. 428.

20. Margaret Malamud, 'Sufi Organizations and Structures of Authority in Medieval Nishapur', pp. 428-9.

integrated into the *madrasas*, and Sufi teachings could be more easily and legitimately broadcast. The Sufi way was becoming an integral part of Islamic culture, devotion and theology.[21]

The extent of ʿAṭṭār's links with these emerging Sufi orders of Nishapur is uncertain; his written works provide few clues on such matters. Many of his shorter lyric poems, however, become more significant if they are seen as didactic or homiletic pieces written for aspiring Sufi novices. Their teaching and exhortation about the mystical path fit well within this didactic context, being suited to an audience of young Sufis.[22] The increasing use and popularity of mystical poetry in the 11th and 12th centuries came partly from the burgeoning Sufi orders' demands for attractive yet instructive poetry.[23] Some of ʿAṭṭār's *ghazals* may well have served in this context, as didactic texts and as poetry for meditation or ritual recitation sessions known as *samāʿ*.

As far as political events are concerned, ʿAṭṭār's lack of regard for worldly affairs may have been guided by more than purely religious or philosophical reasons. It is clear that the overriding importance of mysticism and his retreat into the world of the inner life meant that political or social concerns were of little significance in his life and writings.[24] His lack of concern for worldly affairs and his view of political power as transitory and insubstantial may also be due to the constantly changing, precarious and violent nature of politics in the Seljuq age. The rapidly changing fortunes of rulers, their tenuous grasp on power, and their swift rise and fall may not have been unusual in Iranian political history, but it certainty underscored the fragility and evanescence of striving for secular power.

The arbitrary and personal nature of political power in medieval Persia meant that there was little security in the tenure and authority of administrators and political rulers alike. Even the greatest and most powerful of viziers, Niẓām al-Mulk (d. 1092) was not immune from this. The vizier's office was potentially one of great power, but also of great risk. He had no real security, could be dismissed at the whim of the

---

21. Margaret Malamud, 'Sufi Organizations and Structures of Authority in Medieval Nishapur', pp. 430-1.

22. J.T.P. de Bruijn, 'The Preaching Poet: Three Homiletic Poems by Farīd al-Dīn ʿAṭṭār', *Edebiyât*, no. 9, 1998, pp. 85-100.

23. Julie Scott Meisami, *Medieval Persian Court Poetry*, Princeton, Princeton University Press, 1987, p. 272.

24. See further, Hellmut Ritter, *Das Meer der Seele: Mensch, Welt und Gott in den Geschichten des Farīduddīn ʿAṭṭār*, Leiden, E.J. Brill, 1978, chapter 7.

sultan, and was the object of jealousy by both the sultan and other high officials. Jealousy, intrigue and corruption were the order of the day; the bureaucracy had no tradition of integrity or independence; relatives and clients were appointed to fill key positions, as the spoils of office were shared with retainers and family members. After Niẓām's violent death, the viziers succeeded each other rapidly, and in the late Seljuq period, few escaped murder, prison or the confiscation of their wealth.[25]

'Aṭṭār's lifetime was a period of upheaval and decline in the fortunes of Nishapur, as well as for the political and social situation of the crumbling Seljuq empire. There was a decrease in the central authority of government, with a break-up of various parts of the empire, social and factional struggle within the larger cities, and threats of invasion from outside forces.

Weakening of central authority in Baghdad meant that the *'ulamā'* gained local positions of power, legal, religious, social and economic, aided by the institution of the *waqf* (pious bequest) which absorbed what should have gone in taxes to Baghdad. Thus the vying of the different factions in the Khurāsānian cities, centring around legal/religious differences between the Ḥanafīs and Shāfi'īs, was part of a jockeying for power in more than just religious terms. The leading aristocratic families took part in these struggles, supporting one side or the other. The ordinary people, meanwhile, looked for guidance to the *'ulamā'*, rather than to the discredited government.[26]

Around 1150 the Ghūrid dynasty from a far corner of Afghanistan swiftly rose to power and took control of the former Ghaznavid realm from India to Khurāsān.[27] Their empire just as quickly collapsed and disintegrated about sixty years later, probably all within 'Aṭṭār's lifetime. Here was ample proof, if any was needed, to support his conviction about the transience of worldly power.

'Aṭṭār most likely witnessed the attack on Nishapur by the Ghuzz Turkmen in 1154, when he was probably only a youth. The Ghuzz plundered their way through Khurāsān in their revolt against the heavy-

25. Ann K.S. Lambton, *Continuity and Change in Medieval Persia: Aspects of Administrative, Economic and Social History, 11th-14th Century*, Albany (N.Y.), The Persian Heritage Foundation, 1988, pp. 40-46.

26. Richard N. Frye, *The Golden Age of Persia: The Arabs in the East*, London, Weidenfeld & Nicolson, 1975, p. 216.

27. C.E. Bosworth, 'The Political and Dynastic History of the Iranian World (A.D. 1000-1217)', in *The Cambridge History of Iran*, J.A. Boyle (ed.), vol. 5, Cambridge, Cambridge University Press, 1968, p. 153.

handedness of Sanjar's (reg. 1097-1157) rule. Nishapur's citadel was captured, and the historian Ibn al-Athīr (d. 1233) records that corpses were piled up in the streets. The Ghuzz dragged out those sheltering in the Manīʿī mosque, and burned its famous library.[28]

With the death of the last great Seljuq ruler, Sanjar, in 1157, Khurāsān grew increasingly fragmented as his successors were unable to maintain his strong control over the province. The end of Seljuq power in eastern Iran left a vacuum which invited the intervention of foreign powers and tribesmen such as the Ghuzz and the Khwārazm Shāhs. The collapse of the Seljuqs gave free reign to local factions and sectarian violence. The extent of sectarian feeling, regarded as the curse of Khurāsānian cities, was noteworthy in Nishapur during this period. There was much factional struggle between the opposing Ḥanafīs and Shāfiʿīs which was reflected in political and social turmoil rather than purely religious disagreement. After the Ghuzz onslaught of 1154, for example, some sources claim that each night one of the religious sects would assault a quarter of the city inhabited by an opposing group, with much killing and burning.[29] Again in 1161, the head of the ʿAlid faction was jailed and held responsible for riots and clashes, and the destruction of yet another famous library at the ʿUqailī mosque.[30] During these turbulent decades, agriculture was often disrupted by the trampling of opposing armies and nomad flocks, so that famine resulted. To add to Nishapur's woes, the city was besieged in 1186 and again in the following year as part of dynastic succession struggles.[31]

Besides these political and social disruptions, the city of Nishapur suffered at least two natural calamities during ʿAṭṭār's lifetime in the form of earthquakes, the first in 1145, and the second in 1208.[32]

These circumstances cannot have failed to influence ʿAṭṭār's life and outlook, particularly his view of the vain pursuit of secular power. How he fared during these disruptive events cannot be known directly, though there are some references, especially in his *mathnawīs*, to his disdain of

28. C.E. Bosworth, 'The Political and Dynastic History of the Iranian World (A.D. 1000-1217)', pp. 160-6.

29. A. Bausani, 'Religion in the Saljuq Period', in *The Cambridge History of Iran*, J.A. Boyle (ed.), vol. 5, Cambridge, Cambridge University Press, 1968, pp. 284-5.

30. C.E. Bosworth, 'The Political and Dynastic History of the Iranian World (A.D. 1000-1217)', in *The Cambridge History of Iran*, J.A. Boyle (ed.), vol. 5, Cambridge, Cambridge University Press, 1968, p. 186.

31. C.E. Bosworth, 'The Political and Dynastic History of the Iranian World (A.D. 1000-1217)', p. 190.

32. E. Honigmann (& C.E. Bosworth), 'Nīshāpūr', in *Encyclopaedia of Islam*, vol. VIII, Leiden, E.J. Brill, 1960-, p. 63.

worldly ambitions.[33] It is likely that ʿAṭṭār's rather pessimistic outlook and the sombre tone of his writings was moulded by the distress which he saw around him, as much as by a naturally melancholic temperament.[34]

The unimaginable horror of the Mongol invasion in the early 13th century, their sweep across the eastern Islamic world with terrifying speed and brutality, was a disaster of much greater proportions than the relatively minor disturbances outlined above. The populations of whole cities such as Nishapur were put to the sword, and it is probable that ʿAṭṭār lost his life in this way.

The late 12th and early 13th centuries was a period of increased Sufi activity. Under the early Mongol rulers there was further growth and vitality in the Sufi movement. It may be the case that the search for encounter with God in an intense and private way was a reaction to the grim reality of the Mongol invasions.[35] J. Spencer Trimingham notes that Ghāzān Khān converted to Islam at the end of the 13th century, thereby returning Muslim rule to Western Asia. By this time, the Sufis had displaced the *ʿulamā'* as the representatives of Islam and advocates of the religious life.[36] If the cultivation of spiritual life was the recourse of many during the early Mongol period,[37] ʿAṭṭār's world-transcending attitude anticipated this retreat into the inner realm. His writings as a whole point to the cultivation of spiritual and other-worldly values and actions as the only worthy pursuits of life:

> Since the world's actions are purely ephemeral,
> what is all this frantic search for answers in the world?
> (*Dīwān*, T 106.5)

33. See Hellmut Ritter, *Das Meer der Seele: Mensch, Welt und Gott in den Geschichten des Farīduddīn ʿAṭṭār*, Leiden, E.J. Brill, 1978, especially chapter 7.

34. Pūrān Shajīʿī, *Jihān-bīnī-yi ʿAṭṭār*, Tehran, Ḥaydarī, 1373 a.h.s., pp. 15-6.

35. Ann K. S. Lambton, *Continuity and Change in Medieval Persia: Aspects of Administrative, Economic and Social History, 11th-14th Century*, Albany (N.Y.), The Persian Heritage Foundationm, 1988, p. 322.

36. J. Spencer Trimingham, *The Sufi Orders in Islam*, Oxford, Clarendon Press, 1971, pp. 67,91.

37. Leonard Lewisohn, *Beyond Faith and Infidelity: The Sufi Poetry and Teachings of Maḥmūd Shabistarī*, Richmond, Curzon Press, 1995, chapter 3.

STYLE AND THEMES

The word of Love is nothing but allusion;
Love is not bound by poetic metaphors.
(*Dīwān*, T 110.1)

Since at least the time of the 15th century biographers Dawlatshāh and Jāmī, the name of ʿAṭṭār in the tradition of Persian mystical poetry has been associated with his predecessor, Sanāʾī of Ghazna (d. 1131) and his successor, Jalāl al-Dīn Rūmī (d. 1273). Both Dawlatshāh and Jāmī quote a verse attributed incorrectly to Rūmī, but which links the three poets together:

ʿAṭṭār was the soul[1] and Sanāʾī his two eyes,
we came in the footsteps of Sanāʾī and ʿAṭṭār[2]

Though the genuine source of this verse is obscure, it reflects a widespread view still current today that ʿAṭṭār is the link between the 'first' Sufi *ghazal* writer, Sanāʾī, and Jalāl al-Dīn. Sanāʾī's position in this regard has been shown by J.T.P. de Bruijn as being rather more complex than this simple connection would suggest, not least because this early 12th century writer from Ghazna cannot be accurately described as a Sufi or mystical writer, but rather as a 'homiletic' religious poet.[3] Yet despite some qualifications, a continuing and developing tradition of religious

1. Dawlatshāh Samarqandī, *Tadhkirat al-shuʿarāʾ*, M. Ramḍānī (ed.), Tehran, Khāwar, 1344 a.h.s., p. 75, has 'face'.

2. J.T.P. de Bruijn, 'Sanāʾī and the Rise of Persian Mystical Poetry', *La signification du Bas Moyen age dans l'histoire et la culture du monde musulman: Actes du 8me Congrès de l'Union européenne des arabisants et islamisants*, Aix-en-Provence, 1978, p. 35 ; and ʿAbd al-Raḥman b. Aḥmad Jāmī, *Nafaḥāt al-uns min ḥaḍarāt al-quds*, M. Tawḥīdī Pūr (ed.), Tehran, ʿIlmī, 1375 a.h.s., p. 599.

3. J.T.P. de Bruijn, 'Sanāʾī', in *Encyclopaedia of Islam*, vol. IX, Leiden, E.J. Brill, 1960-, p. 5.

poetry can be seen linking the three writers.

ʿAṭṭār's real achievement in his lyric poetry was to establish the *ghazal* as the main genre of concise mystical expression, and to legitimize its use as an idiom in its own right without the accompaniment of panegyric or other forms of courtly poetry. Unlike Sanāʾī, who might also be credited with establishing this genre, he had no need or desire to write poems of praise, to flatter and appease wealthy patrons. This was both a personal and a literary departure from tradition with a lasting impact, as it paved the way for the later triumphs of Rūmī.

ʿAṬṬĀR AND SANĀʾĪ

Sanāʾī's *Dīwān* is the earliest such collection in Persian to contain a large number of *ghazal*s, just over four hundred in M. Raḍawī's edition. De Bruijn argues that his contribution to the development of the genre lay in giving a new, religious meaning to this form of love and wine poetry. His *Dīwān* is also notable for the many ascetic (*zuhdīyāt*) *ghazal*s and *qaṣīdas*, and a similar number of poems with antinomian themes, known as *qalandarīyāt.*[4] ʿAṭṭār's *Dīwān* has, by contrast, only a handful of *qaṣīdas*, and is dominated by the *ghazal* form. These two writers did not create an entirely new idiom of mystical poetry, but rather shaped the already existing means of expression in new ways. They adapted the forms, images and rhetorical devices known in Persian poetry from as early as the 10th century, as in the quatrains of Abū Saʿīd b. Abī ʿl-Khayr (d. 1049), and used them to express new mystical ideas.[5]

It is difficult not to make broad generalizations about the poetry of ʿAṭṭār when compared with that of his predecessor Sanāʾī, but in reading their *Dīwān*s certain contrasts are apparent. The difference in content of their *Dīwān*s has been noted above, ʿAṭṭār preferring the *ghazal* form while Sanāʾī makes use of a wider range of genres. Jan Rypka describes ʿAṭṭār's lyrics as expressing 'fervent transports of ecstasy',[6] yet these are largely absent from Sanāʾī. What could be described as the mystical-experiential qualities apparent in ʿAṭṭār's poems are not as marked or fully formed in his predecessor's work, while these qualities are even more apparent in Rūmī's *Dīwān*. There is a development from the simpler piety evident in Sanāʾī to the more ecstatic form of mysticism found

4. J.T.P. de Bruijn, 'Comparative Notes on Sanāʾī and ʿAṭṭār', *Sufi*, no. 16, 1992-3, p. 14.
5. J.T.P. de Bruijn, 'Comparative Notes on Sanāʾī and ʿAṭṭār', *Sufi*, p. 19.
6. Jan Rypka, *History of Iranian Literature*, Dordrecht, D. Reidel, 1968, p. 239.

in the later authors. To give an example, Sanā'ī has a preference for the term *'āshiqī*, 'the state of being a lover' (e.g. *ghazals* no. 60; 135.1,2; 139; 244.1,2), but this is seldom used in the absolute, self-giving sense found frequently in 'Aṭṭār's poetry. A notable exception to this is Sanā'ī's *ghazal* no. 60, which expresses ideas more at home with 'Aṭṭār:

Whoever has not pain without end
  has no care for love.

Love is a king with his foot on the throne of eternity,
  except he has no dominion over man.

Love does not enter into reason and knowledge;
  reason and knowledge have no banner for love.

Bū Hanīfa did not teach concerning love;
  Shāfi'ī has no Tradition about it.

Love is living without 'continuance' and 'annihilation';
  lovers have no complaint about it.

Love is a sense beyond what is human;
  water and clay is not sufficient for love.

Whoever has solved the problem of love
  knows that (the solution) is only a guidance.

Love is beneath the subtlety of the unseen world;
  what is that? there is no story about that.

(Compare the similar *ghazal* no.18 in the translations below.)

The similarity between this poem of Sanā'ī and 'Aṭṭār's style shows the close connection between the two.

Sanā'ī is on the whole a rather traditional poet of love, employing the usual features of the now well developed conventions of Persian rhetoric. There is some hyperbole in describing the 'beloved', the usual images of soul and heart, grief and sorrow, but not the exuberance and inspiration of 'Aṭṭār, let alone Rūmī. The hyperbole is measured, as is the mood, which is not as despairing or pessimistic as 'Aṭṭār's often is. The same conventions and images are apparent in both writers, but with 'Aṭṭār there is a more pointed and assured direction and meaning given to these forms. In comparison with the earlier poet, there is more of a feeling of sincere expression and belief in the veracity of mystical language and thought. 'Aṭṭār is, in brief, a more genuinely mystical poet.

THE INFLUENCE OF OTHER EARLIER POETS

Two other poets from the centuries before ʿAṭṭār deserve consideration also. The writings of the colourful Sufi master Abū Saʿīd b. Abī ʿl-Khayr are amongst the earliest examples of Persian Sufi literature available to us.[7] In particular, he is acknowledged as a fluent writer of quatrains, and there is a considerable collection of these which has survived. Though not all of the quatrains attributed to him are likely to be by his hand, these short specimens of poetry contain in germ many of the later themes and images of the classical Sufi tradition. His quatrains deal with the subjects of love and pain, the beauty of the beloved, the yearning of the lover, and so on, in fact the standard repertoire of a Persian poet. Others contain more directly religious themes, such as God's forgiveness, or the day of reckoning, and these might well be described as 'homiletic' poems, to use de Bruijn's terminology. As the first mystical poet in the Persian language, it is perhaps surprising to find that Abū Saʿīd's imagery is well developed and maturely formed. A few examples are in order:

> This is a pain which stole my soul from me;
> this is a love for which no one has the remedy;
> this is an eye which is always shedding blood;
> this is that night which never leads to day for me![8]

> The heart becomes everlasting when it gazes on you;
> grief becomes happiness in its pain for you;
> if the wind carried the dust of your street as far as hell,
> its fire would all become the water of life! [9]

As these examples show, the distance between Abū Saʿīd and ʿAṭṭār, though a century and a half in time, is not nearly as far in poetic terms. In fact the similarities in style suggest that Abū Saʿīd's poetry may well have served as a model for the younger ʿAṭṭār.[10]

The secular poet Niẓāmī Ganjawī (d. 1217?) was a near contemporary of ʿAṭṭār, and his renown and skill makes it likely that he would have been

7. See Terry Graham, 'Abū Saʿīd ibn Abī ʿl-Khayr and the School of Khurāsān', in Leonard Lewisohn (ed.), *Classical Persian Sufism: From its Origins to Rumi*, London, Khaniqahi Nimatullahi Publications, 1993, pp. 83-135.

8. Abū Saʿīd b. Abī ʿl-Khayr, *Sukhunān-i manẓūm*, Saʿīd Nafīsī (ed.), Tehran, Kitābkhāna-yi Sanāʾī, 1349 a.h.s., Quatrain no. 97.

9. Abū Saʿīd b. Abī ʿl-Khayr, *Sukhunān-i manẓūm*, Quatrain no. 180.

10. See Farīd al-Dīn ʿAṭṭār, *Dīwān*, M. Darwīsh (ed.), Tehran, Intishārāt-i Jāwīdān, 1359 a.h.s., p. 10.

an influence on the latter. On looking into Niẓāmī's *Dīwān*, however, we are led to the conclusion that 'Aṭṭār relied only marginally on the secular tradition represented by this contemporary poet. Niẓāmī tends to have a denser style and lacks the lyrical fluidity of 'Aṭṭār. Unlike his renowned epic work, his *ghazals* are not as splendid as the later and more famous Persian lyricists. There is the impression that the great themes of love poetry, made so sublime in the verse of the Sufis, were not felt deeply by Niẓāmī. This view contradicts that of Jan Rypka who argues that Niẓāmī's 'lyrical poems are in fact permeated with passionate emotion and transported into a state of constant ecstasy by an unusual distinction between Thou and I'.[11] A comparison of the two authors shows the great contribution and development made by 'Aṭṭār, who transformed the genre of love lyrics into a vibrant and radiant medium for the expression of mystical ideas and experiences. This contribution is perhaps overlooked when so much attention is focussed on the achievements of Rūmī. Niẓāmī's lyrics do not carry the flavour of religious or mystical passion. He can hardly be condemned for this, if he was not by nature a deeply religious person. Yet it illustrates, by way of contrast, the power of the religious vision, which gives 'Aṭṭār's work its great beauty.

THE INFLUENCE OF ASCETIC POETRY

Among the sources of 'Aṭṭār's style is the tradition of ascetic poetry which first appears in Arabic literature. The earliest genre is the so-called *'Udhrī* love poetry stemming from the seventh century. It is 'a poetry of faithful, chaste and debilitating passion for unattainable objects...[of] passions that led to deep melancholy and often to death'.[12] These poets were given to an obsession, not remembering the past joys of love but deferring consummation permanently, love for these writers being 'a cherished disaster into which one is hurled by fate and which one nurtures with a somewhat ostentatious chastity'.[13] J. Christoph Bürgel and G.M Wickens have noted the influence of *'Udhrī* poetry in Persian literature, with an element of unfulfilled longing and a pessimistic mood as part of the *ghazal*'s stylised vocabulary.[14] Many of these elements are found in

11. Jan Rypka, *History of Iranian Literature*, pp. 212-3.

12. A. Hamori, 'Love Poetry (Ghazal)', in *The Cambridge History of Arabic Literature: 'Abbasid Belles-Lettres*, Julia Ashtiany et al (eds.), Cambridge, Cambridge University Press, 1990, p. 205.

13. A. Hamori, 'Love Poetry (Ghazal)', p. 205.

14. J. Christoph Bürgel, 'Love, Lust and Longing: Eroticism in Early Islam as Reflected in Literary Sources', in A.L. Sayyid-Marsot (ed.), *Society and the Sexes in Medieval Islam*, Malibu,

'Aṭṭār's lyrics, fitting well with the requirements and the temperament of mystical verse. The often obsessive and unfulfilled nature of mystical love is an appropriate subject for this poetry, as is renunciation and the ascetic attitude generally. Hellmut Ritter argues for the importance of the *'Udhrī* influence on 'Aṭṭār's love poetry. The intense emotion and total renunciation of any physical love is part of the heightened, spiritualized poetry which is the voice of 'Aṭṭār.[15]

The other genre of Arabic poetry which shares many of these features and which also influenced the Persian *ghazal* is ascetic poetry proper, *zuhdīyāt*. A similar world-denying attitude is present in this genre, which stemmed from the 8th and 9th centuries. This poetry is associated with early Islamic ascetic movements before these developed into the 'love' mysticism of the early Sufis, exemplified in the famous woman mystic, Rābi'a al-'Adawīya (d. 801).[16] There is a more religious foundation to the world-denying attitude of this poetry, based on Qur'ānic attitudes to renunciation and repentance, which explains the character of this verse.[17] The usual themes include the vanity and transience of earthly achievement; the adoption of *tawakkul* or complete reliance on God and limiting oneself to meagre sufficiency; warning against heedlessness of death and judgement; the ever-presence of mortality, and hence the need for repentance.

Many of these elements are present in 'Aṭṭār's lyrics, though in view of his acknowledged sombreness and pessimism,[18] it is debatable whether this reflects his genuine mood and temperament, or is merely an influence from earlier ascetic models. As in other cases where the question of the poet's genuine expression is weighed against his use of conventional rhetoric, the balance often comes down on the side of personal expression (but see the next subsection of this chapter).

A clear example of the *zuhdīyāt* genre, with the themes of renunciation and preparation for the next world, is provided in the following poem

Undena, 1979, p. 95; and G.M. Wickens, 'Persian Literature: an Affirmation of Identity', in Savory, R.M. (ed.), *Introduction to Islamic Civilization*, Cambridge, Cambridge University Press, 1976, pp. 75-6.

15. Hellmut Ritter, *Das Meer der Seele: Mensch, Welt und Gott in den Geschichten des Farīduddīn 'Aṭṭār*, Leiden, E.J. Brill, 1978, p. 352.

16. Annemarie Schimmel, *As Through a Veil: Mystical Poetry in Islam*, New York, Columbia University Press, 1982, p. 15.

17. A. Hamori, 'Ascetic Poetry (Zuhdiyyāt)', in *The Cambridge History of Arabic Literature: 'Abbasid Belles-Lettres*, Julia Ashtiany et al (eds.), Cambridge, Cambridge University Press, 1990, pp. 265-74.

18. Hellmut Ritter, *Das Meer der Seele*, p. 146.

which has a homiletic or didactic purpose:

For those who have ventured on the path of piety
 their first step is set against the door of the world.

They have turned their back against this nest of demons,
 then like the angels they have turned their faces to the hereafter.

They became freed from the bond-like realms of being,
 they set up for themselves neither possessions nor dwellings.

....

They swore repentance and new vows,
 and for this fresh start they put on the garments of piety.

....

.... (T 295 = N 273)

Such *zuhdīyāt* often have a didactic purpose in ʿAṭṭār's *Dīwān*, and a tone of exhortation.

In the case of a mystical poet such as ʿAṭṭār, there is a suitable correspondence of Sufi themes—unrelenting love, abstinence, repentance, and pessimism about secular values—with the elements of *ʿUdhrī* and ascetic poetry. These earlier genres seem to have evolved very naturally into later Sufi poetry, and ʿAṭṭār's own temperament largely agreed with these elements, as is shown from the evidence of his *mathnawī* writings.[19]

THE CONVENTIONS OF THE *GHAZAL*

It has been noted above that ʿAṭṭār, and Sanāʾī before him, employed the existing styles and conventions of Persian poetry, while adapting them to new ends and imbuing them with the spirit of mystical religion. It is thus the spirit and purpose of the *ghazal* form which changed with ʿAṭṭār's writing, the poetic idiom and means of expression remaining much as before. The poet speaks,for example, of the 'beloved' in a variety of metaphors, as the rose, the moon or the sun; the beloved's 'curls' have exaggerated powers of enchantment; his/her 'face' is shining like the sun. Meanwhile the 'lover' is distraught and madly enchanted, bewailing the beloved's absence, having a heart seared or fevered in longing or distress, and so on.

Despite this adoption of traditional imagery, however, no poet before ʿAṭṭār employed the *ghazal* genre to nearly the same extent, and no other previous writer gave so little attention to the other forms of court poetry,

19. Hellmut Ritter, *Das Meer der Seele*, Chapter 9.

such as the panegyric *qaṣīda.* In part this is due to what was mentioned before about ʿAṭṭār's disdain of traditional courtly poetry with its insincere flattery of wealthy patrons, and outlandish use of hyperbole. ʿAṭṭār's secure livelihood as a pharmacist/physician meant that such a stance could be sustained; he had no need, as well as no desire, to adopt the practices of the professional poet.[20] Yet there is more to this situation than such an explanation provides; there is no real value in disdaining what one can easily dispense with. There is a more genuine reason for ʿAṭṭār's adoption of the *ghazal* as his principal form of concise poetry. This lies in the nature of the genre, its encouragement of personal expression, and its suitability for depicting actual experience of the mystical path.

The problem with this 'personal' view of the *ghazal,* however, is that the extent of the poet's genuine experience being reflected in his work must be weighed against widespread adherence to conventional forms of expression. Many Western scholars argue against the 'personal expression' view and lean towards the overriding importance of tradition. W. Skalmowski, for example, writes that the 'straightforward' approach, which assumes genuine expression of the poet's feelings,

> overlooks the stereotypical character of the ghazal that allowed or even compelled the poets to use the same images and metaphors through centuries without any thematic innovations, a situation hardly compatible with the poets' alleged personal involvement.[21]

Julie Scott Meisami also argues the case for convention, leaving little room for the expression of the poet's personal voice:

> The initial impression of spontaneity, or of "sincerity", produced by its ostensible status as a love lyric that expresses personal emotion gives way, on reading many such poems, to a conviction of its repetitiveness and extreme conventionality.[22]

Meisami argues that the *ghazal* has been misinterpreted as the sounding of the poet's personal voice, and that it shows little real subjectivity. The 'I' of the signature verse (the *takhalluṣ*) functions as 'a deliberately constituted persona—that of the poet-lover, who is simultaneously identified with and distanced from his poem through the agency of the *takhalluṣ*.' [23]

20. Hellmut Ritter, *Das Meer der Seele*, pp. 150-6.

21. W. Skalmowski, 'The Meaning of the Persian Ghazal', *Orientalia Lovaniensia Periodica,* no. 18, 1987, p. 146.

22. Julie Scott Meisami, *Medieval Persian Court Poetry*, Princeton, Princeton University Press, 1987, p. 239.

23. Julie Scott Meisami, *Medieval Persian Court Poetry*, p. 262.

As for the accusation of 'repetitiveness', there may be a better explanation then mere adherence to conventions and stereotyped expression. Farooq Hamid, writing about Rūmī, suggests that in speaking the Sufis' 'unspeakable truth', use of a non-rhetorical verbal structure will not suffice: 'He must create and use such a poetic form that constantly and repeatedly reinforces the nature of his subject matter: the various tenets and purposes of his Sufi vision'.[24] This explanation better accounts for what we might regard as repetitive expression, without having to label the poet a repetitive conventionalist.

It is certainly the case, however, that some of these strictures of Skalmowski and Meisami apply to the *ghazals* in 'Aṭṭār's *Dīwān*. There are occasions where the conventionality, rather than the individuality, of the poet is at the forefront. Yet equally there are many instances where the *ghazal* form expresses directly and forcefully the poet's feelings and moods, though at times these feelings may be filtered through conventional rhetoric and time-worn images. One example is in the frequency with which the poet addresses the 'soul' (*jān*) or 'heart' (*dil*) in what amounts to a form of dialogue between the poet and his self. The traditional rhetoric of love and the lover, his burned or bloodied heart, the soul taking the role of the inaccessible 'beloved', and so on, is found often enough. Yet the poet's own personal expression does not seem hidden by an overload of conventional rhetoric and imagery. It is seldom felt that the individual statement of the poet is not made clearly and that his particular character does not shine through. Thus the Iranian scholar, Pūrān Shajīʿī, writes of the distinction between 'Aṭṭār's lyric poetry and that of his *mathnawīs*. In the former, his *ghazals* are 'words of the heart, and an explanation of its anxieties', while the didactic prose poems depict the journey of the Sufi aspirant through the valley of love.[25]

Perhaps even more important for a Sufi poet such as 'Aṭṭār is the opportunity afforded by the *ghazal* genre to express mystical experience and doctrine. As a didactic tool, and as a means of expressing personal mystical insights, this short poetic form is highly appropriate, and there is evidence that 'Aṭṭār used his poetry for these purposes. The inherent lyricism of the form provided an attractive vehicle for didactic purposes, and this is often seen in the 'homiletic' (to use de Bruijn's term) and openly

24. Farooq Hamid, 'Storytelling Techniques in the Masnavī-yi Maʿnavī of Mowlana Jalal al-Din Rumi: Wayward Narrative or Logical Progression?', *Iranian Studies*, vol. 32, no. 1, 1999, p. 38.

25. Pūrān Shajīʿī, *Jihān-bīnī-yi 'Aṭṭār*, Tehran, Ḥaydarī, 1373 a.h.s., pp. 9-10.

pedagogical style sometimes employed. *Ghazal* no. 43 in the translations below provides a superb example of a didactic lyric which teaches about mystical experience, and is surely aimed at an audience of Sufi novices.

As mentioned in chapter 1, there is no direct evidence of ʿAṭṭār being connected with the nascent Sufi orders of Nishapur. However, the Sufi organisations which were growing in popularity and influence required an increasing supply of suitable literature and poetry for ritual recitation and more direct teaching purposes. This partly accounts for the increasing popularity and availability of Sufi poetry in the 11th century and afterwards, down through the Mongol period, when there was a greater emphasis on spirituality and the inward life.[26] This circumstantial evidence might well explain the significant number of ʿAṭṭār's *ghazals* which have a clear didactic purpose, and which present Sufi teachings in an attractive form.

It is for these reasons that ʿAṭṭār chose the *ghazal* genre as his principal means of succinct poetic expression. It allowed for direct, personal expression, though often employing conventional rhetoric, it allowed for the expression of mystical experience, and it provided an excellent vehicle for the purpose of teaching aspiring Sufis.

WINE IMAGERY

The widespread imagery of wine and drinking employed in ʿAṭṭār's poetry is ultimately derived from the long secular tradition of bacchanalian verse in Arabic and Persian literature. Ehsan Yarshater traces the origins of this verse in Persian to the court milieu of pre-Islamic Iran, the poetry from this period being often concerned with the glorification of wine and drinking.[27] Here is found the formation of 'stock characters' or 'types' associated with drinking, the handsome wine-bringer (*sāqī*), the carefree drinker or dissolute character (*rind* or *qallāsh*), the 'false preacher' warning against drinking, the taverner, and so on.

The employment of such imagery in mystical *ghazals*, apart from being a conventional feature of such poetry, must also be due to the association of mystical experience with drinking and becoming drunk. Reasons for this association are not hard to find, with both drunkenness and the experience of mystical gnosis having common features as types

26. Julie Scott Meisami, *Medieval Persian Court Poetry*, p. 272.

27. E. Yarshater, 'The Theme of Wine-drinking and the Concept of the Beloved in Early Persian Poetry', *Studia Islamica*, no. 13, 1960, pp. 44, 48.

of altered states of consciousness. There are other factors which reinforce this association. Suzanne Stetkevych argues that in Arabic poetry the connection between wine imagery as a symbol of immortality is probably based on Qur'ānic references to paradise as a place where wine flows freely.[28] The famous Arabic wine poem of Ibn al-Farīd (d. 1235) exploits both this connection and the association of 'pre-eternal' wine with the covenant of Alast (Qur. 7.172).[29]

F. Harb has suggested that the imagery of wine and mystical gnosis in Arabic poetry goes back to earlier Christian and other mystical traditions where ecstasy was seen as intoxication.[30] The later association of wine drinking with Christian and Zoroastrian religions is an important one in the imagery of the Persian *ghazal* generally, and with 'Aṭṭār in particular. References to Christian monasteries or Magian temples as taverns and wine houses occur frequently, often with an implied slander on the faith and practices of non-Muslim religions. As wine was forbidden to Muslims, it was assumed that other religions drank to excess, and the association of such drinking with apostasy provided further literary possibilities, as with the link between drinking and mystical consciousness. There were also associations with idol worship and other illicit practices. Such references to non-Muslim religions, apart from being slanderous, are highly fictional and stereotyped. Annemarie Schimmel has suggested that these references display a very superficial understanding of other religions.[31] In any case these multiple associations provide the poet with a wealth of imagery, often of a highly conventional type.

One of the stock characters who appears frequently in 'Aṭṭār's wine *ghazals*, the Magi elder or master (*pīr*), is found at times to represent a Sufi master or *shaykh*. Some poems present a quasi-narrative account of the revered Sufi master who enters the tavern, sometimes to castigate the drinkers there, only to succumb to their offer of wine which affords the reception of gnosis and spiritual awakening. *Ghazal* no. 6 in the translations provides an excellent example of this type, the 'master'

28. Suzanne Pinckney Stetkevych, 'Intoxication and Immortality: Wine and Associated Imagery in al-Ma'arrī's Garden', in Wright, J.W.(jr), and Rowson, Everett K. (eds.), *Homoeroticism in Classical Arabic Literature*, New York, Columbia University Press, 1997, pp. 210-232.

29. See R.A. Nicholson, *Studies in Islamic Mysticism*, Cambridge, Cambridge University Press, 1921; repr. 1980, Chapter 3.

30. F. Harb, 'Wine Poetry (Khamriyyāt)', in *The Cambridge History of Arabic Literature: 'Abbasid Belles-Lettres*, Julia Ashtiany et al (eds.), Cambridge, Cambridge University Press, 1990, pp. 233-4.

31. Annemarie Schimmel, *Stern und Blume: Die Bilderwelt der persischen Poesie,* Wiesbaden, Harrassowitz, 1984, p. 94.

speaking as the narrator:

Early one morning I went to the tavern
to beseech the drunkards to obey God.

....

....

[a drunkard] gave me some wine;
my mind faded; I left superstition behind.

As I vanished from my frayed life
I found myself in union with the Beloved...

....

There are a number of variations on this general theme, one of which is the master's apostasy and adoption of the antinomian faith of a *qalandar*.[32] This antinomian element also shows itself in brief references to outspoken and unconventional Sufi figures from the past, identifying them as 'master'. Figures represented here include Abū Yazīd al-Bisṭāmī (d. 874), Shiblī (d. 946), and especially Ḥallāj who was martyred in 922. Ḥallāj, for whom ʿAṭṭār felt a special affinity, is specifically mentioned as a 'master' who drinks the wine of gnosis, experiences awakening, adopts infidelity, and is led to his death. Underlying these poems is the correlation of drinking wine with mystical experience, and of proclaiming heretical beliefs in the public preaching of Ḥallāj's radical views.[33]

ʿAṭṭār's *ghazal*s often express this paradox of wine and drinking being associated with mystical experience on the one hand, and with accusations of impropriety, infidelity or censure on the other (but see further the subsection below on Qalandarīyāt).

MYSTICAL THEMES AND SYMBOLISM

The increasing use of mystical themes and metaphors in ʿAṭṭār's poetry has been noted, the older secular conventions being transformed by him and given new meanings and references. It is significant that Jan Rypka mentions ʿAṭṭār's 'infectious enthusiasm'[34] as one of his chief characteristics,

32. See further J.T.P. de Bruijn, 'The Qalandariyyāt in Persian Mystical Poetry, from Sanā'ī Onwards', in Leonard Lewisohn (ed.), *The Legacy of Medieval Persian Sufism*, London, Khaniqahi Nimatullahi Publications, 1992, pp. 75-86.

33. See further Kenneth Avery, 'The Theme of the Sufi Master and the Tavern in the Lyric Poetry of ʿAṭṭār', *Sufi*, no. 48, 2000/01, pp. 8-13.

34. Jan Rypka, 'Poets and Prose Writers of the Late Saljuq and Mongol Periods', in *The Cambridge History of Iran*, vol. 5, J.A. Boyle (ed.), Cambridge, Cambridge University Press, 1968, p. 590.

while on the other hand his pessimistic mood and sombreness has also been acknowledged.[35] These are probably the two sides of the one coin, as his exuberant mood alternated at times with a darker temperament. This also demonstrates the extent of the poet's personal voice being expressed through the conventional vehicle of *ghazal* poetry.

The sources of the mystical themes and symbols used by 'Aṭṭār are far-reaching and multifaceted, being the literary, cultural and religious history of the Persian Sufis. It is not possible to catalogue them all here, but merely to mention some of the most important.

i) Imagery from the Qur'ān

Qur'ānic references and symbols are among the most widely used, perhaps not surprisingly by a Sufi poet. Such references are usually not made directly to the Qur'ānic text itself, but are filtered through understandings derived from a long and diverse history of mainstream exegesis, *tafsīr*, and Sufi interpretation, *ta'wīl*. Such early commentary as that attributed to Ja'far Ṣādiq (d. 765), or the exegesis of Muqātil b. Sulaymān (d. 767), 'Abd al-Raḥman al-Sulamī (d. 1021), and the more widely known Sahl al-Tustarī (d. 896)[36] developed a terminology and interpretative framework which paved the way for later writers. The luxuriant development of imagery and symbolism connected with the Qur'ān meant that later writers were able to give the merest allusion in order to tap into this enormous reservoir of traditional spiritual lore and teaching. One example of this rich development is with the symbols associated with 'historical' figures, such as Moses or Abraham. For Sufi exegetes, and hence for later poets, such figures are often transformed into idealized 'lovers' of God, or into a *walīy*, 'friend' (of God) or 'holy man' of a distinctively Sufi character. Moses' receiving of the revelation on Sinai becomes a personal mystical encounter; he becomes 'a paradigmatic mystical figure because of his dramatic confrontation with God'.[37] Conversely, Pharaoh becomes a paradigm for the obstacles of earthly existence, or the impedance of the lower, carnal soul or *nafs*. An example

35. Hellmut Ritter, *Das Meer der Seele*, p. 146.

36. See Paul Nwyia, *Exégèse coranique et langage mystique*, Beirut, Dar el-Machreq sarl, 1991; and John Burton, 'Quranic Exegesis', in M.J.L. Young et al (eds.), *The Cambridge History of Arabic Literature: Religion, Learning and Science in the 'Abbasid Period*, Cambridge, Cambridge University Press, 1990, pp. 40-55.

37. Carl W. Ernst, *Rūzbihān Baqlī: Mysticism and the Rhetoric of Sainthood in Persian Sufism*, Richmond, Curzon Press, 1996, p. 62.

of this opposition occurs in *ghazal* no. 6 of the translations (T 17;N 14):

....

As I vanished from my fayed life
    I found myself in union with the Beloved.

As I was freed from the Pharaoh of being
    I became Moses at the chosen mountain.

....

The allusion to the revelation to Moses from Qur. 7.142ff is already in the exegesis of Ja'far Ṣādiq interpreted as a spiritual encounter. The Qur'ānic 'appointed place' is glossed by Ja'far as 'the quest for seeing [God]'.[38]

An example of the didactic *zuhdīyāt* or 'ascetic' genre mentioned previously illustrates the profusion of such imagery which can occur within a few short lines:

....

They [the ascetics] killed the Pharaoh-soul with spiritual disciplines,
    then they placed their hearts on Moses' fire.

When they took to the path with the parrots [of heaven],
    [they cried:] 'hail to them!', for they were set at the top of the *ṭūbā* tree.

As a viaticum for the journey and provisions for this fearful valley,
    they placed their severed head on a salver like John the Baptist.

Firstly they became dust beneath the feet of dogs,
    lastly like the wind they bowed their head to their Lord.

'Aṭṭār whose words gave life to the soul,
    found that Jesus became their companion.

(T 295 = N 273)

The *ṭūbā* is not actually mentioned in the Qur'ān as a tree in paradise, but the image is built on an allusion in Qur.13.29 meaning 'prosperity' or 'blessedness'. Later, under the influence of a prophetic *ḥadīth* (sacred Tradition), and the mention of other trees in heaven, it came to be understood as a tree of paradise where birds or parrots perch.[39] Again there is no direct mention of John the Baptist's violent death in the Qur'ān, but later tradition came to annex the Christian story concerning him.

38. Paul Nwyia (ed.), 'Le Tafsīr mystique attribué à Ǧa'far Ṣādiq', *Mélanges de l'Université Saint-Joseph*, vol. XLIII, no. 4, 1968, p. 196.

39. See *Tafsīr Jalālayn* and *Tafsīr Ibn Kathīr*, Qur. 13.29.

ii) Philosophical Themes

Other types of motif occurring in 'Aṭṭār's *ghazals* are what could be defined as philosophical or metaphysical themes. Such philosophical writings, rather than being lyrical or love-poems, most likely served as didactic or homiletic pieces, with the purpose of teaching Sufi aspirants. Often these poems are lengthy, and deal with such topics as the mystical 'creation' of the world, the relation between God and other forms of being, the nature of the self and the soul, or the workings of God's marvellous light. As poetry, its topics are probably more akin to the *qaṣīda* form with its longer length and ability to sustain single themes.

This genre contains poetry which is among the most difficult to understand of all 'Aṭṭār's work, as the following examples illustrate:

> When you unite your soul to the Source of sources, without yourself,
> then you are you without your self for that you-ness is hidden from you.
>
> This you-ness is a part in regard to the carnal self, but all in regard to the heart;
> yet you are neither this nor that, rather both are that reality of you.
>
> In this there is you, and in that; how do you ever reach [the real] you?
> for your Source is outside your carnal soul and your higher soul.
>
> .... (T 41 = N 47)

Such subtle and ambiguous expression often eludes understanding, though here a distinction maintained between the real or essential self as against the lower, unreal self (*nafs*) helps explain these verses.

One of the most brilliant, if succinct and cryptic, of this genre is *ghazal* no.12 of the translations. A similar *ghazal* is the following, which treats the subject of existence and non-existence:

> While all people, high and low, are imagining you,
> it is forbidden to breathe a word about love.
>
> While each and all have not yet become one,
> it is common to claim unity with you.
>
> Until you have become free of your existence,
> every existing ripeness is raw.
>
> Since the source of all is definitely no existent [like us],
> this [Being] is nothing incomplete like all other [existents].
>
> Seek the source, pass by the derivatives,
> for the latter is ephemeral, the former eternal.
>
> .... (T 81 = N 74)

A final example of this genre deals creatively with the imagery of light and darkness:

....

There is a path to the sun for each atom;
    without a doubt each atom became a claimant.

Good and evil are like the reflection of your face and hair;
    one became light diffusing, the other rained darkness.

The darkness of your face found it made denial;
    the rays of your face shone and became acceptance.

Whoever was worthless fell into darkness;
    and whoever upheld truth became filled with light.

The essence of light came from experiencing the Light of light.
    the essence of darkness came from the grief of [Hell-] fire.

.... (T 252 = N 234)

iii) Qalandarīyāt

One of the constantly recurring themes in 'Aṭṭār's *ghazal* poetry is that known as the *qalandarīyāt* motif, the expression of outlandish, immoral and irreligious behaviour and attitudes. The persona of the poet or the subjects of his poem claim unbelief and adopt impious practices, drinking wine, gambling and dancing, and associating with non-Muslims (Christians or Zoroastrians) in taverns or 'ruins' beyond the fringes of society. The Sufi systematizer Shihāb al-Dīn Suhrawardī (d. 1234), a near contemporary of 'Aṭṭār, coined the phrase 'destruction of conventions' to describe the attitudes of those who adopted this code in real life.[40] This tendency among mystics, also known as *malāmatīya*, 'those seeking to bring blame on themselves', had strong associations with the province of Khurāsān, and with Nishapur in particular, as early as the ninth century.[41] The outward show of piety and asceticism and its popular approbation was seen as running counter to the true aims and motives of the mystical path. The solution to this religious paradox was to conceal one's devotions and even to appear outwardly reprehensible and invite

---

40. J.T.P. de Bruijn, 'The Qalandariyyāt in Persian Mystical Poetry, from Sanā'ī Onwards', in Leonard Lewisohn (ed.), *The Legacy of Mediaeval Persian Sufism*, London, Khaniqahi Nimatullahi Publications, 1992, p. 76.

41. J.T.P. de Bruijn, *Persian Sufi Poetry: An Introduction to the Mystical use of Classical Persian Poems*, Richmond, Curzon Press, 1997, p. 72; and Alexander Knysh, *Islamic Mysticism: A Short History*, Leiden, Boston, Köln, Brill, 2000, pp. 94ff.

censure on one's actions. Whether the literary expression of this attitude had much correspondence with real life behaviour, however, remains a point of contention.[42]

As a poetic form this *qalandarīyāt* genre is widespread in ʿAṭṭār's poetry. In his classification of themes in the *Dīwān*, Ritter emphasised the presence of this motif, perhaps to the exclusion of other important elements.[43] In this context, de Bruijn has raised the question of the genuineness of the poet's feeling in expressing 'reprehensible' motifs, compared to his mainstream belief and practice. De Bruijn argues that we should be warned 'not to read a reflection of reality in these poetic images'.[44] He suggests that both Sanāʾī and ʿAṭṭār were not irreligious or antinomian, but were pious Muslims who accepted the conventions of Islam. It is not so clear cut, however, that these two apparent polarities cannot coexist. The piety and faith of ʿAṭṭār involves the rejection of worldly success and its false values, the abandonment of life and the willingness to accept death for the sake of the Beloved. It is difficult to affirm that these deeply held beliefs and attitudes which are so pervasive in his poetry could be only literary fictions or masks. Ritter adopted the view that the *qalandar* poems are probably a purely literary genre, and that poets such as ʿAṭṭār and Sanāʾī had devoted themselves to such a life only in fantasy. Yet this does not alter the fact that the poems are a reflection of actual Sufi practice.[45]

This paradoxical situation is perhaps best illustrated by the contrast often portrayed between the falsehood and hypocrisy of the ostentatious ascetic and the genuine 'piety' of the *qalandar* or antinomian mystic. The ascetic who makes a public display of his piety is seen as acting contrary to the real purpose of the Sufi way which is the quest for the state of love.[46] The antinomian or apparently irreligious mystic is paradoxically the one who is most genuine in his quest for love since he has abandoned all desire for approbation in the present world. This is expressed most clearly in the opening *ghazal* of ʿAṭṭār's *Dīwān* (translation no.1) where these two attitudes are contrasted:

---

42. J.T.P. de Bruijn, *Persian Sufi Poetry*, p. 75.

43. Hellmut Ritter, 'Philologika XV Farīduddīn ʿAṭṭār III.7. Der Dīwān', *Oriens*, no. 12, 1959, pp. 1-88.

44. J.T.P. de Bruijn, *Persian Sufi Poetry*, p. 75.

45. Hellmut Ritter, *Das Meer der Seele*, pp. 490-1.

46. J.T.P. de Bruijn, *Persian Sufi Poetry*, p. 72.

Since there is no one to be our companion in Love
the prayer-mat is for the pious; wine-dregs and vice for us.

A place where people's souls turn and twist like polo balls
is not a place for rogues; so what's that got to do with us?

If the wine-bringers of the spirit sit with the devout
their wine is for the ascetics; lees and hangovers for us.

.... (T 1 = N 1)

Similar themes are found in T 392 = N 353:

O pious ascetics! Show you have a heart which is awake!
[you] are all drunk; show one of you to be sober in thought!

Do not make any claim, if you are worthy of faith;
show yourself in the bazaar as you are within [your hearts]!

I can show thousands making claim from the mosque;
show one worthy to know mysteries outside the taverner's!

....

iv) Secular Mythology

Somewhat paradoxically 'Aṭṭār makes use of secular Persian heroes and myths found in the works of Firdawsī and Niẓāmī. Unlike these secular poets, however, he incorporates figures from the *Shāh-nāma* and other Persian sources in an Islamic mystical framework, sublimating their non-religious epical or picaresque origins and connotations. Thus we find mention of the legendary kings Jamshīd and Khusraw, heroes such as Siyāwush and Rustam, in allusions to their mythological deeds, but transcended through religious symbolism.

NATURE AND THE IMAGINATION

'Aṭṭār is above all a poet of the heart and the imagination, not a writer who engages with the outer world of the senses. This observation comes as no surprise, and it is largely true of most Sufi poets that the inner world is much more important than the external.

In an analysis of Rūmī's style, much of which might apply to 'Aṭṭār, Robert M. Rehder argues that there is no careful observation or description in this poetry. There is no elaboration, and no actual reference to or location in the external world. There is only psychological observation and concern with inner events; the 'lover' is self-absorbed, looking toward the soul and the spirit.[47] This lack of interest in looking at the world is related to the poet's belief that the external world is in a state of flux and its real nature cannot be observed. In its place the poet offers 'the universe of phantasy', as coined by Rehder, an imaginal world where all is possible in a process of endless change and constant transformation of metaphors. Each poem is a moment or unit of thought, expressing feelings at their highest pitch in an ecstasy of words.[48] In a similar vein, Ritter suggests the presence in ʿAṭṭār's poetry of 'dream-like' sequences, with the beloved standing for God, particularly when the poet's soul is the arena of action.[49]

It is usual in ʿAṭṭār's *ghazals* to find a lack of interest with the external world, though there are some eloquent exceptions of fine nature poetry. The following example (no. 21 in the translations) is a hymn of praise to the dawn:

Pour a cup of morning draught; the dawn has arrived.
It has drawn its sword to sever the head of night.
....
The sweet scent of dawn is musky as though
it has tasted the musk of a Chinese deer's tail.
.... (T 151 = N 143)

It is true of ʿAṭṭār, as de Bruijn has argued in relation to Sanāʾī,[50] that descriptions of nature are not meant to be realistic, but rather they depict an ideal world in stylised form. These idealised descriptions have symbolic connotations made explicit when their function in the poem is considered. The beauty of nature in spring or the decay and melancholy of autumn, for example, reflect the changing fortunes of the lover. This use of figurative and symbolic forms requires a tacit understanding of referents between poet and audience.[51]

It is also true that ʿAṭṭār looks inward for his inspiration and is self-absorbed, partly for the reasons mentioned by Rehder, the changeability, unreality and lack of value of the external world. This is expected with mystical poets whose source of knowledge and creativity is their inner

47. Robert M. Rehder, 'The Style of Jalāl al-Dīn Rūmī', in Chelkowski, P.J. (ed.), *The Scholar and the Saint*, New York, New York University Press, 1975, pp. 276-7.

48. Robert M. Rehder, 'The Style of Jalāl al-Dīn Rūmī', pp. 279-84.

49. Hellmut Ritter, 'Philologika XV Farīduddīn ʿAṭṭār III.7. Der Dīwān', p. 52.

50. J.T.P. de Bruijn, *Of Piety and Poetry: The Interaction of Religion and Literature in the Life and Works of Ḥakīm Sanāʾī of Ghazna*, Leiden, E.J. Brill, 1983, pp. 189-90.

51. J.T.P. de Bruijn, *Of Piety and Poetry*, p. 215; and W. Skalmowski, 'The Meaning of the Persian Ghazal', *Orientalia Lovaniensia Periodica*, no. 18, 1987, pp. 141-162.

world. The action in this poetry takes place in a spiritual world where heart (*dil*) and soul (*jān*) are the main players. The dramas concern 'love' often as an abstract concept, the 'lover'-heart/soul, and the beautiful but cruel 'beloved'. These roles and persona are often interchanged in a constant metamorphosis of imagery.

THE POETRY OF LOVE

Outlining the features of this triangular relationship allows a better understanding of the *ghazal*'s structure. The 'lover' is usually 'I' or 'us', the persona of the poet. In the *takhalluṣ* or final signature verse, however, this persona is referred to in the third person, as though the poet addresses himself from a distance, or perhaps in a mirror. The 'beloved' is usually addressed in the second person as 'thou', or sometimes as a more distant third person. Since the Persian language allows for no gender distinction in second or third person verbs or pronouns, the gender of the 'beloved' remains ambiguous. Despite this, male gender is usually assumed, evidently deriving from the early history of the *ghazal* as part of court entertainment for male gatherings and drinking parties, stemming from pre-Islamic times.[52] Thus we find the male wine-server (*sāqī*), the youthful, newly bearded court servants, and male minstrels/reciters. (In our translations, however, we have preferred a female beloved for reasons given in chapter 4 below.) In the more abstract and less sensual poetry of the mystical *ghazal*, there is usually a sublimation of these figures, and a more introspective discourse. The poet's inner self (*jān* or *dil*) may be addressed as second or third person.

In reference to the courtly origins of love poetry, Julie Scott Meisami argues for an intimate link between the concept of love on the one hand, and princely society and its ideals on the other. In this view there is a parallel between the lover's stance and that of the poet-courtier, between the lover's suit and the poet's desire to further his position and gain influence and rewards.[53] Yet as Meisami also points out, this courtly conception of love contrasts strongly with the 'obsessive but self-immolating love' of the early Arabic *'Udhrī* poets. It was argued earlier in this chapter that the spirit of the *'Udhrī* poets, their unfulfilled longing and pessimism, is clearly evident in 'Aṭṭār's *ghazals*. It would seem that

52. E. Yarshater, 'The Theme of Wine-drinking and the Concept of the Beloved in Early Persian Poetry', *Studia Islamica*, no. 13, 1960, pp. 43-53.

53. Julie Scott Meisami, *Medieval Persian Court Poetry*, Princeton, Princeton University Press, 1987, p. 28.

these earlier sources, which included the rich tradition of the archetypal or legendary Arab lovers, *Majnūn* and *Laylā*, were more influential for 'Aṭṭār than the ideals of court society.[54] There is little of the courtly milieu in 'Aṭṭār's poetry beyond those 'internalized' influences which were common to the Persian tradition, such as the figures of the wine-bringer or the newly bearded youth. These stock figures are in any case subsumed into the symbolism of mystical expression, and retain few of their original characteristics. The notion of poetry as a courtly drama where the poet-lover advances his suit in hope of increasing his wealth and prestige is anathema to all which 'Aṭṭār held dear.

The pessimism and self-denial of *'Udhrī* and ascetic poetry has been noted above as an important element in 'Aṭṭār. Yet because the *ghazal* is essentially a love lyric, this gives rise to a paradox: 'Aṭṭār's lyrics are concerned mostly with the pain and suffering of love, and are better described as laments. The ideal paradise of unity and intimacy with the beloved alternates with the actual inferno of the poet's feelings, of rejection, degradation, taunting and exile from the object of his love. In fact the quest for joy and intimacy with the beloved is also the source of the lover's constant grief and pain, of rejection and separation. It is this latter state which dominates, as few *ghazals* speak of the joys of unity and intimacy. This is acknowledged in a reflection on his poetry in the final verse of T 220 = N 199:

> Why did you not caress me like a harp? for 'Aṭṭār
> brought forth a lament like a high pitched string with each breath.

In terms of mysticism, this pain so often expressed by Sufi poets is explained by M. Lings as reflecting the contradictory condition of 'the relative' that has been touched by 'the absolute', the finite opened to the infinite. The only cure for this anxiety-causing condition is 'another touch, another opening'.[55] 'Aṭṭār writes:

> The remedy for love of the beloved is also constant pain for him;
> do not seek a remedy for the heart if the heart lives by pain.
> (T 776)

The heart is a restless 'sea', the depths of the poet's inner self, the source of his poetry and of his understanding of the world:

54. As'ad E. Khairallah, *Love, Madness and Poetry: An Interpretation of the Mağnūn Legend*, Beirut, Franz Steiner Verlag, 1980.

55. M. Lings, 'Mystical Poetry', in *The Cambridge History of Arabic Literature: 'Abbasid Belles-Lettres*, Julia Ashtiany et al (eds.), Cambridge, Cambridge University Press, 1990, p. 240.

When ʿAṭṭār's heart became a sea of love,
many were the jewels we scattered from his tongue.
(T 602 = N 543)

This source and creative inspiration is at once the inner world so often spoken of in his verse, and at the same time a mirror of the world at large. For the mystic, these two apparent worlds are one; there is no separation between inner and outer, which is why the imagery of the poet's 'universe of phantasy' so easily and quickly alternates between both realms. In a similar vein, Ritter argues that there is no necessary distinction between heavenly and earthly love or beauty. In this poetry there is a strong relationship and close connection between the two, and a theoretical dichotomy between symbolic and actual is not helpful for our understanding.[56]

THE DIVINE AND THE SOUL

The realization of the oneness of God and the human soul is the aim of human life and the mystic quest. But whereas this goal of realization may perhaps be seen as akin to the Hindu identity of *ātman-Brahman*, it is in fact the unity of a lover with his Beloved. Rather than being the dispassionate, changeless single principle of the universe, God is the overwhelmingly beautiful Beloved for whom every human soul longs, and in this longing all human desires and emotions, suffering and joy are directed. This insight which is the expression of direct mystical experience, is the basis and motivation for ʿAṭṭār's poetry.

At the centre of this universe is the One, the divine 'You', the Beloved, the Hidden Treasure of the soul, known by a myriad of other descriptions:

O my Soul of soul of soul, You are the Soul of soul of soul;
outside the soul of soul, what is there? You are That and more than That!
(T 813)

This quote from the *Dīwān* illustrates one of the main conceptual fusions in ʿAṭṭār's poetry, or indeed in any other genuine mystical writing. There is an apparent ambiguity or indistinctness about the subject being addressed. Is the poet here speaking in a type of monologue to his own soul, or is he addressing the divine Beloved, the Soul as we might say? A translation into a modern European language must choose between upper or lower case, Soul or soul, Divine or non-divine. In Persian (or

56. Ritter, *Das Meer der Seele*, op.cit., p. 436.

Arabic, Hebrew, Sanskrit etc.) such a choice is not required because of the nature of the script, and hence a referential fusion is allowable.[57] It seems that the Divine may be addressed in a whole variety of ways, as alluded to above, by a multiplicity of ultimately inadequate names or descriptions. The poet's essential self, in Persian his *jān*, is but one of the 'subjects' of this address, being the intersection or convergence between the human and the Divine. Yet this is an inadequate explanation too, since the poet's whole world is subsumed into the world of God, the only Reality. There is no other Reality than the Divine, a fact of Sufi experience which goes well beyond the mainstream Islamic statement of belief:

> You see all of Him, since all is eternally Him;
> in both worlds there is not anything outside of the Friend.[58]

> See with the soul that all you see is Oneness;
> the person who became effaced saw through the eye of the soul.
> Since both worlds arose from one jewel,
> [the person effaced] saw many mines in a tiny jewel.
> He found eternity without beginning and end to be a drop [of water];
> he saw both being and place as the placeless.
> (T 379 = N 345)

The mystic whose eye 'sees' by means of *jān* discovers the true nature of the universe, the divine Oneness and the unreality of the physical world. God being the only reality means that nothing else has any separate or essential existence:

> Whoever rests with one atom of being
> kneels to worship each atom.
> ....
> ....
> In fact since everything is the One
> every being is nonexistent.
> (T 338 = N 297; see below the *ghazal* in full translation, no. 38)

The external world is seen as lacking real existence, and yet all being is subsumed under the One Reality. This is related to, and partly explains, the problem mentioned above about the uncertainness of the subject

57. Michael A. Sells, *Mystical Languages of Unsaying*. Chicago and London, University of Chicago Press, 1994, p. 10.

58. Farīd al-Dīn ʿAṭṭār, *Muṣībat-nāma* ed. Nūrānī Wiṣāl. Tehran, Zawwār, 1380 a.h.s., p. 134, line 1.

being addressed in many poems. If the divine Beloved is apparent in a myriad of created forms, then the poet should tend to look outward at this created world for the imagery and inspiration of his verse. Yet as we have seen, like all mystics he looks inward; indeed he rejects the outer world, finding the essence of what is real in his own *jān*. The *jān* is the microcosm of the divine, and hence there is this alternation between the utterly transcendent yet omnipresent One and the utterly personal 'soul' which is a mirror of the transcendent. Moreover, the constant refrain of 'Aṭṭār's poetry is to look inward at the divine reality of the *jān*. In the very next verses following on from the last verse quoted above, the poet writes:

The unconscious is the source of fire.
 What's to gain from watching the smoke?

In the eyes of those who see the source
 both worlds immediately disappear.

When the two worlds are seen with the heart's eyes
 they are like a mirage, devoid of substance.

What use is it to see the smoke of the fire within and not to see the fire itself? Such images, particularly of fire and of sea, constantly appear in these calls to discover the inner world.

Though the *jān* is the microcosm of the divine world, this does not allow humans to become 'divine' or for the indwelling (*ḥulūl*) or fusion of the two natures, an idea attributed to Christian doctrine or Gnostic mysticism:

It's not possible for any creature
 to turn God-like or become the Creator.

But a truthful thing could be said
 if the essence and quality of the self fade.

Every time one becomes annihilated from these two,
 He will subsist in the essence of Oneness.

The Presence in speaking of this state says:
 A person does not become Us but becomes of Us.

(T 176 = N 164; see translations, no. 22)

Ritter argues that this notion of being annihilated and sustained in God, the favoured Sufi polarity of *fanā'* and *baqā'*, is not a static monism where the chief aim is the disappearance of false knowledge and the adoption of true gnosis. 'Aṭṭār's 'system' is more dynamic, since annihilation in God is a real process, not an intellectual or gnostic understanding. This annihilation is also a cosmic process involving the disappearance of all things save God, based on Qur'ān 28.88: 'All things perish save His face'.[59] Being is conceived as a sea, from which all things derive and to which all things return; *fanā'* or annihilation is entering into this sea, to which the reader is often exhorted by the poet, and *baqā'* is existence in this Sea of Being.[60]

THE POET ON HIMSELF: THE MOTIVE OF HIS WRITING

In his study of 'Aṭṭār's *mathnawīs*, Ritter attempts the hazardous undertaking of discovering the motives for the poet's writing. It is true that the poet's primary mood is one of sadness and pessimism, and that the poet is self-critical of his squandered opportunities and his unhappiness about being a poet.[61] Having kept away from courts and princes, the poet's complaint is that of loneliness; he has deliberately distanced himself from the occupation of *qaṣīda*-writing and court poetry generally. The resulting loneliness, despair, and absence of sympathetic friends as well as his irrepressible desire to speak, form the motives which induced 'Aṭṭār to write.[62]

It is not always the case, however, that the poet speaks transparently about his own situation. In the epilogues of his *mathnawī* works, and occasionally in the last verse of a *ghazal*, 'Aṭṭār tends to boast of his own literary achievements in a rather immodest style. Despite his alleged self-criticism, loneliness and perplexity, he still speaks with pride of his own creations, and of his originality. Despite his protestations about not wishing to be regarded as a poet, he indulges in these formal and conventional paeans of self-praise. His self-disclosures about his motives for writing, therefore, should not be taken at face value.

In a different context, however, Ritter argues that in the forefront of the poet's work is the desire to rid everyday contentedness and apathy from people's minds, to highlight the restlessness of the heart, to create a desire for higher aims and to extol the virtues of sorrow and grief.[63] These aims are certainly applicable to the poet's *ghazals*, for they contain

59. Hellmut Ritter, *Das Meer der Seele*, p. 612.
60. Hellmut Ritter, *Das Meer der Seele*, p. 637.
61. Hellmut Ritter, *Das Meer der Seele*, p. 146.
62. Hellmut Ritter, *Das Meer der Seele*, pp. 150-6.
63. Hellmut Ritter, *Das Meer der Seele*, p. 248.

this deep sense of restlessness and aspiration for transcendent values. This fundamental character of the poet's verse betrays his motives, perhaps more than his formal and conventional words about himself. Annemarie Schimmel writes of the incessant thirst and longing for the divine which motivates the writing of religious poets:

> It is this thirst that made the poets create. Words die when union has finally been achieved, but the never-ending yearning for the beloved made talkative those who were well aware that mystical experience cannot properly be communicated through words.[64]

64. Annemarie Schimmel, *As Through a Veil: Mystical Poetry in Islam*, New York, Columbia University Press, 1982, p. 79.

THE LEGACY OF 'AṬṬĀR'S POETRY

'Aṭṭār's writings have long been regarded as the birthplace of Persian Sufi poetry. His fusion of concepts as seemingly divergent and incompatible as courtly love poetry and ascetic mysticism, Qur'ānic motifs and *qalandarī* imagery, can be seen as the genesis of much Sufi poetry in the following centuries. It could be argued that had it not been for his radical and innovative use of the *ghazal*, this poetic form may not have achieved the popularity and prevalence it has enjoyed ever since in Iranian literature and world poetry.

1) RŪMĪ

Legend has it that the aged 'Aṭṭār gave a copy of one of his books, the *Asrār-nāma* (*Book of Secrets*) to the young Rūmī who was fleeing with his family from Balkh on route to Konya in about 1215. If there is lasting significance in this story it is that 'Aṭṭār bequeathed a great poetic legacy to the younger and ultimately more famous writer. 'Aṭṭār had already prepared the path by developing the existing *ghazal* genre and imbuing it with a transcendent spirituality which produced extraordinary poetry conducive to sublime faith. Rūmī took advantage of the fact that the mystical lyric *ghazal* was fully formed and ripe by the time of his writing, or rather by the time of his ecstatic recitation, if the traditions concerning his mode of composition are acknowledged.[1]

Many similarities in style and language can be found in the poetry of both authors, and it is to 'Aṭṭār's credit that he originated many of these ideas and forms. Some of these similarities have been recognized in the

1. See A.J. Arberry, *Mystical Poems of Rūmī*, Chicago and London, University of Chicago Press, 1968, Introduction.

notes to the poems translated below, but on a more general level there is one overriding correspondence which should be mentioned here.

It cannot be overstated that both authors were non-systematic thinkers and writers; at heart they were both poets first and foremost, rather than philosophers or theologians. Robert M. Rehder argues the case for Rūmī, that as an unsystematic author, his thought cannot be separated from its poetic expression. There is not an elaboration of a philosophy, but an attempt to understand experience; abstractions are never stable, but they become metaphors, or personifications, or undergo other changes; there are no conclusions, only other poems.[2] This characterization applies similarly to 'Aṭṭār. As essentially intuitive writers of poetry, whether in the *mathnawī* couplet form, or in the lyric genre of the *ghazal*, their work is imbued with a deep mystical sense. They attempt to understand and explain the spiritual dimension, in which the processes of reasoning intellect, or the 'bindings of the mind' (*'aql;* using Michael Sell's expression[3]), play a minor role.

There are, however, a number of differences in the style of these two poets. 'Aṭṭār's lyrics are closer to the origins of the *ghazal* genre in earlier courtly poetry. This influences the adoption of bacchanalian imagery associated with wine drinking and the tavern. As has been mentioned earlier, this imagery is analogous to altered state experience and conversion to unconventional faith. While there are many examples of such imagery in Rūmī's *Dīwān*, there is a more direct and conscious application in 'Aṭṭār's poetry. For Rūmī, this imagery is well integrated as an accepted part of the poetic tradition, with the sense of there being a greater distance from its courtly origins.

This leads to the observation that the analogical sense (to use Julie Scott Meisami's terminology[4]), the integration of microcosm and macrocosm, inner and outer, part and whole, is more strongly established in Rūmī's lyrics. Instead of perceiving resemblances, as with the use of metaphor, analogical comparison assumes a continuity between the outer and inner worlds. This continuity pervades Persian, and particularly Sufi, poetry, and with the two poets discussed here it is perhaps more a difference of degree rather than of kind.

2. Robert M. Rehder, 'The Style of Jalāl al-Dīn Rūmī', in Chelkowski, P.J. (ed.), *The Scholar and the Saint*, New York, New York University Press, 1975, pp. 282-3.

3. Michael A. Sells, *Mystical Languages of Unsaying*, Chicago & London, University of Chicago Press, 1994, p. 111.

4. Julie Scott Meisami, *Medieval Persian Court Poetry*, Princeton, Princeton University Press, 1987, pp. 30ff.

A further important difference is that of the mood and temperament of the two poets. It is generally acknowledged that Rūmī's poetry conveys a great sense of exaltation, elation and rapture. It is said that he composed his poetry in an ecstatic state, and that this accounts for its spontaneity and lack of regard for exact style.[5] However this may be, his *ghazals* exude a sense of joy, hope and wonder at the place of the mystic lover within the divine Beloved's cosmos. ʿAṭṭār, on the other hand, displays a much more sombre and melancholy outlook in his poetry. Hellmut Ritter argues that pessimism is ʿAṭṭār's primary mood, embracing his self-criticism for lost opportunities, sadness over his life as a poet, and a consequent alternation between agnosticism and despair.[6] In his lyric poetry this pessimism is expressed in the fundamental theme of the unattainability of the divine Beloved. This is the most often occurring motif in the whole *Dīwān*, and the basis for much of his poetry. In terms of mainstream Islam, it reflects the unbridgeable distance between God and humankind. Allied to this theme of unattainability is a belief in the necessity of grief and pain in this world, displayed in the poet-lover's endless suffering recounted constantly in poem after poem. For Rūmī, these same existential facts of humankind's situation give rise to the joy of attainment to the Beloved, and of exaltation and wonder at the Creator's world.

2) ḤĀFIẒ

In 1959 Hellmut Ritter wrote a valuable article comparing selected poems of ʿAṭṭār with those of Sanāʾī and Ḥāfiẓ.[7] The later poet from Shiraz is one of the most celebrated figures in Persian literature, at the forefront of *ghazal* writers, who helped make this genre the most sublime expression of the Persian poetic voice. The development of this genre, from ʿAṭṭār through Rūmī to Ḥāfiẓ, is not difficult to chronicle, and Ritter summarises the differences between the earlier poet of Nishapur and his counterpart from Shiraz.

Much scholarly discussion has occurred in the latter half of the 20th century concerning the perceived lack of unity in many of Ḥāfiẓ'

5. Annemarie Schimmel, *Stern und Blume: Die Bilderwelt der persischen Poesie*, Wiesbaden, Harrassowitz, 1984, p. 8.

6. Hellmut Ritter, *Das Meer der Seele: Mensch, Welt und Gott in den Geschichten des Farīduddīn ʿAṭṭār*, Leiden, E.J. Brill, 1978, p. 146.

7. Hellmut Ritter, 'Philologika XV Farīduddīn ʿAṭṭār III.7. Der Dīwān', *Oriens*, no. 12, 1959, upon which much of this section is based.

ghazals.[8] That this question has absorbed mostly Western rather than native Iranian scholars is perhaps more indicative of the preconceptions which Westerners have about Persian literature. However this 'problem' is resolved, Ritter assumed the lack of thematic unity in Ḥāfiẓ, and saw this as a real difference from ʿAṭṭār's lyrics. He observed a stronger unity and connectedness of thought in the earlier poet, in contrast to the kaleidoscopic style of Ḥāfiẓ.[9]

A more pertinent difference, however, was the contrasting mood and tone discernible in the two poets. ʿAṭṭār has a more earnest, serious, even melancholic style, as he deals with transcendent themes and mystical problems, as well as the anguish of his heart. The mood of Ḥāfiẓ, on the other hand, is more even-tempered and invariable, serene and with a scent of gaiety, humour and mischief. There is often a wavering double entendre about whether his love poetry refers to earthly or divine love, or whether the wine songs are representations of real or mystical experience.[10] This teasing quality, which is a constant of Ḥāfiẓ' style, is completely absent in the earlier poet. With ʿAṭṭār we are sure of his real intent, of his sincerity as a religious poet. This leads Ritter to conclude that Ḥāfiẓ cannot be regarded as a genuine mystical poet.[11] Yet this in no way detracts from Ḥāfiẓ' brilliance, or his originality, and, as with Niẓāmī, he is not diminished for not being sincerely religious.

ʿAṭṭār certainly lacks the dazzling virtuosity of the later poet. The now stereotyped themes of wine, rose and nightingale appear more frequently in Ḥāfiẓ' work, perhaps due partly to his writing in a later century, and the conditioning of the poetic language which had occurred in the intervening years. One also has the feeling that as a genuinely spiritual poet, ʿAṭṭār is constantly attempting to find new and more appropriate expression for his inner experience. With Ḥāfiẓ, on the other hand, we are often uncertain of his real intent; the reader is always being teased and seduced by the subtlety and brilliance of his poetry, as he expresses himself in virtuosic language often for its own sake.

3) SYMBOLIST INTERPRETATION

A problematical approach to interpreting ʿAṭṭār is that of the later

8. See particularly Michael C. Hillmann, *Unity in the Ghazals of Hafez*, Minneapolis: Bibliotheca Islamica, 1976.

9. Hellmut Ritter, 'Philologika XV Farīduddīn ʿAṭṭār III.7. Der Dīwān', pp. 2,20.

10. Hellmut Ritter, 'Philologika XV Farīduddīn ʿAṭṭār III.7. Der Dīwān', pp. 8,9,14.

11. Hellmut Ritter, 'Philologika XV Farīduddīn ʿAṭṭār III.7. Der Dīwān', p. 56.

symbolist tradition which seeks to explain Sufi poetry in terms of the 'transconscious realm of archetypal meanings'.[12] Mystical-symbolic exegesis or *ta'wīl*, such as that of Shabistarī and his famous commentator Lāhījī, may well apply to later, post-Ibn ʿArabī poetry, since the Andalusian master himself wrote a paradigm for this exegesis with a *ta'wīl* on his own *Tarjumān al-Ashwāq* (*Interpreter of Desires*).

It is a literary anachronism, however, to read later, symbolist interpretation into earlier poetic traditions. The earlier poetry is understandable in its own terms, as love lyrics with meanings pointing to a mystical reality, but not with every image being an anagogic metaphor of the archetypal realm of esoteric significance. It is conceivable that some such meanings can be discovered in the early writings, but much of this poetry has a more direct and substantial reference which cannot be ignored. The early poetry was in a constant state of development and adaptation from previous secular, courtly genres. As the symbolist school tends to ignore or gloss over this historical development, an anachronistic 'reading back' into earlier writers is made possible. If the evolutionary development of Persian Sufi poetry is not acknowledged, the question has to be asked why the poets adhered to the basic imagery of the earlier, secular courtly writers. Why, then, was it necessary to 'spiritualize' every aspect of traditional imagery, with every expression requiring a supra-mundane layer of exegesis? In fact, why write poetry at all, if every word is symbolic of a highly refined theosophical system better expressed in philosophical prose? The logical application of this system renders as nonsense what is in fact a genuine art form and a cry from the poet's heart.

A further problem with the symbolist approach is the rigidity of definition, of strict denotation between the ordinary language of the poem and its archetypal meaning. Once an image or metaphor is assigned its supra-sensual reference, it is given a straightjacket which restricts its allusive power and its ability to serve in a variety of poetic contexts. The question must also be asked as to who 'defines' these archetypal referents. It is seldom the poet, Ibn ʿArabī being an exception here, but usually it is later commentators or lesser poets influenced by the original writer, or a Sufi 'master' who may or may not understand the poet's intention. Not only does symbolism deny the historicity of Sufi poetry, it also stifles

12. Leonard Lewisohn, *Beyond Faith and Infidelity: The Sufi Poetry and Teachings of Maḥmūd Shabistarī*, Richmond, Curzon Press, 1995, p. 183; and see the criticism of the symbolist school by Julie Scott Meisami, *Structure and Meaning in Medieval Arabic and Persian Poetry: Orient Pearls*, London and New York, RoutledgeCurzon, 2003, pp. 49-50.

critical reappraisal by later interpreters by rendering fixed and sterile a particular interpretative mechanism. The poet's original language is thus frozen by the symbolist school's insistence on a single, rigid '"re-assignation" of poetic images back to their original noumenal Object'.[13]

Any analysis which seeks to interpret poetry without a primary literary-critical focus fails to do justice to this special form of discourse. If poetry is not seen firstly as a literary form, it becomes a theosophical text, and is read primarily as theology or philosophy, not as literature. Though ʿAṭṭār's *Diwān* contains valuable theosophical material, his writing is primarily poetic in nature, and as we have mentioned above, he is, like Rūmī, a poet rather than a systematic thinker.

4) THE LEGACY OF ʿAṬṬĀR.

The unsatisfactory alternatives for the interpretation of Sufi poetry, between the romanticizing tendency adopted by earlier Western scholars, such as A.J. Arberry, and the symbolist approach discussed above, are not the only possibilities available. Each of these approaches has something to offer, despite the limitations of the symbolist school, but both are only partially adequate.

The romantic school tends to emphasize purely literary and poetic concerns, which are indeed important, but which underplay any considerations of function and context. The Sufi poet is seen as a radical outsider, a freethinking libertine in the mould of Fitzgerald's Omar Khayyām, with his poetry being a romantic cry far from the constraints of Islamic society and mainstream religion.

A third approach might be attempted. This would be to incorporate the literary-critical insights of the romantics with the mystical vision of the symbolists. One also needs to seek out the psychology behind these poems, and look at their function and context within ʿAṭṭār's society, and after his death. We have attempted something of this approach in the present study, though perhaps with limited success.

Exploring the psychology behind these poems is fraught with difficulty. As argued in the introduction, the individual expression of the poet is often drowned in the traditional language of stereotyped imagery. It is our belief, however, that the poet's genuine voice can still be heard in most instances. His temperament, his melancholy and occasional despair, his pessimism at the unattainability of love, and his reluctance to play the

13. Leonard Lewisohn, *Beyond Faith and Infidelity*, p. 196.

part of a poet are all keenly felt, and we are seldom left with no idea of his expressed feeling.

The function and context of ʿAṭṭār's poetry is also somewhat problematic, as we have no direct evidence of its use or circulation. It is likely, however, that it served in mystical circles, in Sufi orders and lodges, or in more formal contexts as both teaching material, and as recitation texts for *samāʿ* or formal recital sessions. As teaching material, many of the *ghazals* are well suited, some being openly didactic or exhortative in tone, content and form. It is easy to see how such poems could be used to teach Sufi novices and aspirants on the mystical path. Other poems which are not so obviously didactic could also have served as inspiring and enjoyable teaching material, providing a new and attractive means of spreading spiritual teachings and ideas. As recitation texts, these *ghazal*s were also well suited, showing the natural genius of the poet in exploiting the resources of the Persian language. ʿAṭṭār used many of the classic linguistic devices such as polysemy, homophony, word plays, and so on, not for their own sake, but to emphasize and enliven his message.

To conclude, the following quote from Taqī Tafaḍḍulī, the editor of the *Dīwān*, is apposite:

> ʿAṭṭār had no concern with poetry or the profession of poet; in his eyes it had no value, and he was not happy to be counted as a poet. He had no thought of metre or rhyme schemes, and knew himself more as a mystic concerned only with spiritual realities. Despite all this, he is truly and justifiably known as one of the most eloquent and stylish poets of the Persian language.[14]

14. Farīd al-Dīn ʿAṭṭār, *Dīwān*, Taqī Tafaḍḍulī (ed.), Tehran, Bungāh-i Tarjama u Nashri Kitāb, 1967, p. 25.

ON TRANSLATING THE *GHAZALS* OF 'AṬṬĀR

In his seminal 1923 introduction to his German translation of Baudelaire's *Tableaux Parisiens*, the thinker and literary critic Walter Benjamin contemplates 'the Task of the Translator'.

He begins by defining two types of 'bad translations'. The first type is what is often considered to be 'faithful': it aims at nothing other than simply transmitting information from one language into another. The second type could be considered as the first type's binary opposite: it is 'poetic' or 'free'; and functions as poetry in 'its own right'.

Why are these types of translation both 'bad'? One answer may already be evident: the 'faithful' translations, due to focusing on only the *content* (information) of the original, are bound to completely ignore the *aesthetics* of the original, resulting in often ineffective deformations such as 'prose translations of verse'. The second, 'creative' approach often results in a 'new' poetry that, to establish 'its own right', inevitably excludes and displaces the original, a phenomenon all too familiar to the readers of modern revisions of, among others, Homer, Dante and, most recently, Rūmī.

So what is a 'good' translator of poetry to do? Benjamin first defines the *intention* of a language (or 'pure language') as something that a poet *intends* or *desires* to express via a 'tongue'. According to Benjamin, recognizing this intention, which constitutes the 'kinship of languages',[1] is the translator's foremost task:

> The task of the translator consists in finding that intended effect

1. Walter Benjamin, *Illuminations*, trans. H. Zohn, London, Fontana, 1992, p. 74.

> [*Intention*] upon the language into which he is translating which produces in it the echo of the original.[2]

In other words, the task of a translator is to neither convert nor transform an original poem, but to write something that *echoes* the original poem; that is, something that reverberates, and repeats without imitation, the intended effect or discourse of the original. Therefore the two works, while disparate in many evident ways (e.g. 'tongue', form, even content), must share the very same intention, the very same 'pure language'.

We should therefore discuss our translations of 'Aṭṭār's poetry in terms of the *intended effect* of the language of his *ghazals*; a language that is neither the tongues of medieval Persian (in the originals) nor contemporary English (in our translations); but the 'pure language' of an esoteric discourse.

While Sufism is usually considered as an Islamic 'mysticism', the poetry associated with this tradition is often not ascetic, puritanical or directly religious.

For example, as even a casual reader of Rūmī, Ḥāfiẓ and, indeed, 'Aṭṭār would have noted, these poets' works are literally saturated with, if not direct representations of, then unapologetic allusions to carnal love, debauchery, 'binge' drinking, and an ambivalent attitude towards Islam. Even to date any discussion of the evident (homo)sexuality of Rūmī's *Dīwān of Shams* would arouse nothing short of ire among conservative circles; and, according to a traditional story, the clergy not only harassed Ḥāfiẓ during his life, they also denied his body burial due to his 'blasphemous' *ghazals*.

But describing Sufi poetry as merely 'controversial' speaks of the poems' *affect* and not their *intention*, and does not serve as a poetics for translating them. Therefore we should focus on the genre of Sufi poetry as a discourse, and explain the reasons for having called it an *esoteric discourse*.

Firstly, by 'discourse' is meant a communication as well as a dissertation; that is, saying something and arguing for or against what is being said at precisely the same time; or, as philosopher Michel Foucault would have it, 'a series of discontinuous segments whose tactical function is neither uniform nor stable'.[3] In other words, the functions of expressing

2. Walter Benjamin, *Illuminations*, p. 77.

3. Michel Foucault, *The History of Sexuality: 1 – The Will to Knowledge*, trans. R. Hurley, London, Penguin, 1990, p. 100.

an idea and explaining (often with the aim of defending) that idea are clearly different things and not continuous or uniform. The first aims at a definition, the second at *dis/empowering* that definition, but, within a discourse as such, a number of ideas are put forward and are, as Foucault would have it, reinforced, exposed and undermined while the idea is being put forward.[4]

Central to a discursive reading of Sufi poetry, and 'Aṭṭār's original *ghazals* in particular, is an awareness of the textual opposition between 'us' and 'them'. As can be noted in the very first *ghazal* in this volume, for example, the poet's spiritual ideas—e.g. being in *'ishq* (*Love*) with God, adopting a *rāh* (*Path*) towards a Union with the *ma'shūq* (*Beloved*), etc. —are expressed (via symbolism) as preferable to those of the poet's most persistent Others i.e. ordinary mainstream Muslims. Yet, throughout the poems, this bias is itself undermined by the *depictions* of these symbols and ideas. The *'ishq* is often depicted as an unrequited and even ruinous infatuation; the *ma'shūq* as a temperamental, if not basically irresponsive and cruel, love interest; and the *rāh* as an immensely difficult, and at times impossible, journey.

Is 'Aṭṭār's a paradoxical or even oxymoronic discourse? Is his intention one of irony, even satire? Very unlikely since, as mentioned before, a discourse is always already self-contradictory. What makes 'Aṭṭār's poetry distinct, and brings us to call it 'esoteric', is that it is very *self-consciously* and unreservedly a poetry of contradiction. As could be seen in the conclusion to the first *ghazal*, for example, both the speaker's *andūh* (*sorrow*) and his *andūh-gusār* (*sorrow-undoing* or *solace*), two absolute linguistic opposites, are unambiguously cited as identical features within the same verse.

Such an approach, an awareness of the symbiotic relationship between opposites, the interdependence between them, and their inevitable, if somewhat delayed, assimilation into each other seems to be the very intention of 'Aṭṭār's poetry. As philosopher Jacques Derrida (who coined the term 'deconstruction' for such an approach) may have it, in 'Aṭṭār's poetry there is no difference between sorrow and solace; between *baqā'* (*survival*) and *fanā'* (*annihilation*); *paydā'ī* (*appearance*) and *pinhānī* (*hiding*); *dīn* (*faith*) and *kufr* (*unfaith*); but a 'differance'(sic.), that is, a 'deferment' of the eventual unification of the temporary opposites.[5]

---

4. Michel Foucault, *The History of Sexuality: 1 – The Will to Knowledge*, p. 101.

5. See Jacques Derrida, *Of Grammatology*, trans. G. C. Spivak, Baltimore, Johns Hopkins University Press, 1976.

This idea is best illustrated by one of 'Aṭṭār's central concepts, *The Seven Valleys of Love* outlined in his allegorical narrative poem *Manṭiq al-ṭayr,* and employed throughout his *ghazal*s. Even the seemingly most irreconcilable opposition between Separation and Union, the very paradigm of opposition, is to be dissolved in the quest for Love, in the symbolic depiction of a theologically unfathomable union between one (Being) and the 'Great Other' (God).

As with Derrida, 'Aṭṭār's discourse of deconstruction strives to demonstrate this non-difference between supposed opposites through word play and use of double-entendres. For example, the Persian word for pain, *dard*, is written identically to *durd* (*wine-dregs*). While the two words are phonetically different, they are absolutely indistinguishable as written text. Yet 'Aṭṭār consistently uses these words in the same poem, often within the same verse, to highlight the interchangeability between their meanings; to suspend the opposition between 'pain' and a drink that is supposed to 'ease pain', an idea that seems very close to Derrida's definition of *pharmakon* as both poison and cure.

The very same relationship also exists between the Persian words *gul* (*flower*) and *gil* (*mud*); and once again, 'Aṭṭār uses these words in each other's proximity, without making a clear distinction between which one is which, in order to repudiate the difference between desirable (flower) and undesirable (dirt); between living (plant) and nonliving (earth); and between nature (flower) and *human* nature (clay).

The correlation between 'Aṭṭār's and Derrida's discourses constitutes the aforementioned Benjaminian 'kinship of languages'; and it is this very discourse that we have sought to recognize in 'Aṭṭār's *ghazal*s and echo in our translations of them.

Yet, we call such a discourse 'esoteric' instead of deconstructive, not only because applying a term invented by a 20th century 'post-modern' European thinker to the work of a 12th-13th century Middle Eastern 'mystical' poet seems too crass a modernization (or Europeanization), but also because a term such as 'deconstruction', and the discourse we have been discussing, are, more than anything else, almost unfathomable and, 'in real terms', possibly impenetrable.

One may question, for example, if there is any 'real use' for such an ideology: It may be well and good for a 'mystical poet' like 'Aṭṭār to philosophize that the difference between opposites is illusive and arbitrary; but can the same be said in 'real life'? Can we claim, without resort to 'theoretical' theses of 'relativists' such as Derrida, that there is no difference between life and death, between the living and the non-living, between sorrow and solace?

Our answer, and perhaps 'Aṭṭār's, is that there is no task more 'real' and exigent than precisely questioning the imposed distinctions between such fundamental concepts of life and death, good and evil, right and wrong, etc. 'Aṭṭār's poetry has the intended effect of not only challenging but profoundly disturbing the perceived notions of happiness, love and faith. His was not a poetics concocted in isolation from the 'real world', but one developed in direct response to the dogmas, injustices and, in fact, the 'theories' dominating his world. His and other Sufi poets' challenge to conventional Islam and their search for an ideology and, in fact, a *spirituality* that would reconcile/heal the schisms/wounds inflicted upon their lives is neither 'relativist' nor 'philosophical' but, we believe, nothing short of revolutionary.

Yet, admittedly, this intention of the poet is not spelt out as a polemic, but communicated via symbols, metaphors, metric verse and other trappings of lyric poetry. It is for this reason that we chose to call his approach an esoteric one. While there is absolutely nothing absurdist or 'relativist' about the poems' discourse, they do not convey their meaning/s in particularly lucid 'prosaic' language. In their persistent merging of opposites and forcing their reader to imagine the unimaginable, 'difficult' as they may prove for some, these poems are neither abstract nor ironic, but esoteric attempts at conveying an undeniably difficult, but absolutely crucial, spirituality. It is this discourse that we have tried to echo and reproduce in these translations of selected *ghazals* of 'Aṭṭār.

Here one should also briefly note our approach in translating the gender of the Beloved from the gender-ambiguous Persian nouns, pronouns and adjectives in 'Aṭṭār's poetry. This particular aspect of our work was especially challenging, as 'Aṭṭār's Beloved is clearly not a sexed human but, simply put, a figurative description of the Creator; and English is, of course, a distinctly gender-conscious language.

We finally decided in favour of the feminine in order to maintain the conflation of visceral motifs with metaphysical ideals, a co-existence of opposites that is the hallmark of Sufi poetry. Despite their apparent unconventionality, the Sufis still adopted the *tropes* of medieval love poetry. In this genre, the Beloved as a character type is often a beautiful, haughty and 'unattainable' young woman. Similarly, 'drinking wine' is a *symbol* of transcending mundane rationalism, and yet at the same time an *image* of physical intoxication *and* of the altered state experience of mystical consciousness. Thus we decided that the Beloved should not only be depicted as a symbol of divine, unearthly love, but also simultaneously be an image of an attractive woman and/or female muse.

This decision, and the likes, may seem more interpretive than representative of 'Aṭṭār's poetry, but we hope these translations here still echo the great poet's intended discourses and his enduring messages.

TEXTS AND TRANSLATIONS

I

چون نیست هیچ مردی در عشق یار مارا   سجاده زاهدان را درد و قمار ما را

جایی که جان مردان باشد چو گوی گردان   آن نیست جای رندان با آن چکار مارا

گر ساقیان معنی با زاهدان نشینند   می زاهدان ره را درد و خمار ما را

درمانش مخلصانرا دردش شکستگانرا   شادیش مصلحانرا غم یادگار ما را

ای مدّعی کجائی تا ملك ما ببینی   کز هرچه بود درما برداشت یار مارا

آمد خطاب ذوقی از هاتف حقیقت   کای خسته چون بیابی اندوه زار مارا

عطّار اندرین ره اندوهگین فروشد   زیرا که او تمامست انده گسار مارا

1

Since there is no one to be our companion in Love
    the prayer-mat is for the pious; wine-dregs and vice for us.

A place where people's souls turn and twist like polo balls
    is not a place for rogues; so what's that got to do with us?

If the wine-bringers of the spirit sit with the devout
    their wine is for the ascetics; lees and hangovers for us.

Cure is for the purists, consternation for the broken,
    joyfulness for the do-gooders; while grief is our remembrance.

O pretender, you are not here to witness our wealth
    as the Beloved extorted all that we owned within us.

Words of experience came from the messenger of truth:
    O weary, as you make your way, shed your grief for us.

ʿAṭṭār was absorbed in sorrow along this Path.
    Because he's absolutely finished, his solace is with us.

2

ز زلفت زنده می دارد صبا انفاس عیسی را
ز رویت میکند روشن خیالت چشم موسی را
سحر گه عزم بستان کن صبوحی در گلستان کن
به بلبل می بر داز گل صباصد گونه بشری را
کسی باشوق روحانی نخواهد ذوق جسمانی
برای گلبن وصلش رها کن منّ و سلوی را
گر ازپرده برون آیی وما را روی بنمایی
بسوزی خرقهٔ دعوی بیابی نور معنی را
دل ازما می کند دعوی سر زلفت بصد معنی
چو دلها در شکن دارد چه محتاجست دعوی را
بیک دم زهد سی ساله بیك دم باده بفروشم
اگر در باده اندازد رخت عکس تجلّی را
نگارینی که من دارم اگر برقع براندازد
نماید زینت و رونق نگارستان مانی را
دلارامی که من دانم گر ازپرده برون آید
نبینی جز به میخانه ازین پس اهل تقوی را
شود در گلخن دوزخ طلب کاری چو عطّارت
اگر در روضه بنمایی بما نور تجلّی را

2

Your curls' breeze revives Jesus' breath;
your face's glow reveals Moses' vision.

Head for the garden to drink dew at dawn;
the breeze reports the flower to the nightingale.

Spiritual yearning revokes physical craving.
Desire the Beloved; reject the manna and quails.

If only you'd emerge from behind the veils
to burn the cloak of pretence and deliver the truth.

My heart demands the touch of your curls
but with hearts in each hair, what need for mine?

I'm abstinent for thirty years, but I'll become a wine-seller
should you reflect your splendour in my cup.

If my Beloved would throw aside the veils
Mānī's gallery would be splendidly adorned.

If my Beloved would raise the veils
you'd see only the pious at the tavern.

In the pits of Hell 'Aṭṭār will be in your debt
if you'd shine us your glory from Heaven.

3

گر سیر نشد ترا دل از ما — یك لحظه مباش غافل از ما
در آتش دل بسر همی گرد — مانندهٔ مرغ بسمل از ما
تر می گردان بخون دیده — هر روز هزار منزل از ما
چون ابر بهار می گری زار — تا خاك ز خون کنی گل از ما
آخر بچه میل همچو خامان — گه گاه بگیردت دل از ما
یا در غم ما تمام پیوند — یا رشتهٔ عشق بگسل از ما
مگریز ز ما اگر چه نامد — جز رنج و بلات حاصل از ما
کز هر رنجی گشاده گردد — صد گنج طلسم مشکل از ما
عطّار در این مقام چونست — دیوانهٔ عشق و عاقل از ما

3

If your heart hasn't had enough of us
        please don't ever be heedless of us.

We're snared by the flames of heart,
        making such a slaughtered bird of us.

Vision is shedding tears of blood;
        each day we move a thousand times.

Like a spring cloud you weep bitterly
        and the blood makes the soil muddy for us.

In the end, which of your novice desires
        willy-nilly sicken your heart of us?

Either become one with our suffering
        or detach the strings of love from us.

Don't flee from us, even though there's been
        nothing but pain and disaster for us.

Every pain breaks open the seal
        of talismans keeping the wealth from us.

'Aṭṭār isn't in this state
        just mad with love; he's the sanity in us.

4

در دلم افتاد آتش ساقیا ساقیا آخر کجائی هین بیا
هین بیا کز آرزوی روی تو بر سر آتش بماندم ساقیا
بر گیاه نفس بند آب حیات چند دارم نفس را همچون گیا
چون سگ نفسم نمکساری بیافت پاك شد تا همچو جان شد پر ضیا
نفس رفت و جان نماند و دل بسوخت ذره‌ای نه روی ماند و نه ریا
نفس ماهم رنگ جان شد گو بیا نفس چون مس بود و جان چون کیمیا
زان بمیرانند ما را تا کنند خاك ما در چشم انجم توتیا
روز روز ماست می در جام ریز می می جان جام جام اولیا
آسیا پر خون بران از خون چشم چند گردی گرد خود چون آسیا
خویشتن ایثار کن عطّار وار چند گوئی لا علّی و لا لیا

4

My heart's on fire, O wine-bringer.
O wine-bringer, where are you then? Come on!

Come on. The desire to see your face
keeps me among the flames, O wine-bringer.

A plant's survival depends on water.
I have a soul very much like that plant.

Like a dog, when my soul is nourished
it's tamed, it's a life filled with radiance.

Breath stops, life's extinct and heart burns;
nothing's left of either status or pretence.

My self changed colour to life, as if
self was copper and life alchemy.

It brought our death, and turned us from
dust into celestial antimony.

Today is our day, so pour the wine;
the wine of life into the cup of the saints.

Fill the millstone with the eyes' blood
and yourself spin, spin like the millstone.

Sacrifice yourself like 'Aṭṭār
and chant: *This is not for me or mine.*

5

چه‌شاهد یست که باماست‌در میان‌امشب   که‌روشنست‌زرویش‌همه‌جهان‌امشب
نه‌شمع راست شعاعی نه‌ماه را تابی   نه‌زهره‌راست‌فروغی‌در آسمان‌امشب
میان مجلس ما صورتی همی تابد   که‌آفتاب شد ازشرم او نهان‌امشب
بسی‌سعادت‌از‌این‌شب‌پدید‌خواهدشد   که‌هست‌مشتری‌وزهره‌راقران‌امشب
شبی‌خوشست‌وز‌اغیار نیست کس‌برما   غنیمتست ملاقات دوستان امشب
دمی‌خوشست‌مکن‌صبح‌دم‌دمی‌مردی   که همدمست‌مرا‌یار مهربان‌امشب
میان ما وتو امشب کسی‌نمی گنجد   که‌خلوتیست‌مرا‌باتو در نهان‌امشب
بسازمطرب‌از‌آن‌پرده‌های شورانگیز   نوای تهنیت بزم عـاشقان امشب
همه حکایت مطبوع درد عطّارست   ترانهٔ خوش شیرین مطربان امشب

5

Such a beauty has visited our night
that the world is lit by her face tonight.

No need for either candles or moonlight,
nor for Venus' light in the heavens tonight.

In our gathering her face shines, so
the sun is shamed and hides away tonight.

Such happiness ensues from this dusk
Venus and Jupiter are conjunct tonight.

Such joy, with no foes in our party
meeting friends is the reward tonight.

Don't let this bliss awake by the cruel dawn
for I'm intimate with a kind friend tonight.

No one can come between you and me now
for our solitude is concealed by the night.

Minstrel, play your passionate tunes;
play the song of praise for lovers tonight.

All the story is stamped by 'Aṭṭār's pain;
the sweet songs of the minstrels tonight.

6

سحر گاهی شدم سوی خرابات	که رندانرا کنم دعوت بطامات
عصا اندر کف و سجاده بردوش	که هستم زاهدی صاحب کرامات
خراباتی مرا گفتا که ای شیخ	بگو تا خود چه کارست از مهمات
بدو گفتم که کارم توبهٔ تست	اگر توبه کنی یابی مراعات
مرا گفتا برو ای زاهد خشك	که تر گردی ز دُردی خرابات
اگر یك قطره دُردی بر تو ریزم	ز مسجد بازمانی وز مناجات
برو مفروش زهد و خود نمائی	که نه زهدت خرند اینجا نه طامات
کسی را اوفتد برروی، این رنگ	که در کعبه کند بت را مراعات
بگفت این و یکی دُردی بمن داد	خرف شد عقلم و رست از خرافات
چو من فانی شدم از جان کهنه	مرا افتاد با جانان ملاقات
چو از فرعون هستی باز رستم	چو موسی می‌شدم هردم بمیقات
چو خود را یافتم بالای کونین	چو دیدم خویشتن را آن مقامات
بر آمد آفتابی از وجودم	درون من برون شد از سماوات
بدو گفتم که ای دانندهٔ راز	بگو تا کی رسم در قرب آن ذات
مرا گفتا که ای مغرور غافل	رسد هرگز کسی هیهات هیهات
بسی بازی ببینی از پس و پیش	ولی آخر فرومانی به شهمات
همه ذرات عالم مست عشقند	فرو مانده میان نفی واثبات
در آن موضع که تابد نور خورشید	نه موجود و نه معدوم است ذرات
چه می گویی تو ای عطّار آخر	که داند این رموز واین اشارات

6

Early one morning I went to the tavern
to beseech the drunkards to obey God.

With staff in hand and prayer-mat on shoulder
I was a pious worker of miracles.

One of the drinkers said to me: *O Shaykh*
tell us what's so important at this hour.

I told him: *I'm here to make you repent.*
If you repent you'll gain divine succour.

He told me: *Go away, you dry ascetic!*
Go get wet on the tavern's wine-dregs!

If I sprinkle one drop of wine on you
you'll abandon your mosque and your prayers.

Don't go selling your faith, your vanity;
your virtue won't buy obedience here.

To me you look like the type of person
who'd worship idols in the Kaaba!

Saying this, he gave me some wine;
my mind faded; I left superstition behind.

As I vanished from my frayed life
I found myself in union with the Beloved.

As I was freed from the Pharaoh of being
I became Moses at the chosen mountain.

As I found myself above both worlds
I saw myself among the noble ranks.

Such a sun emerged from within me
I was turned inside out in the heavens.

I said to him: *O knower of mysteries,*
tell me when I'll reach my Beloved.

He said to me: *You ignorant fool!*
Does anyone ever 'reach'? Never! Never!

You may play your games forever
but in the end you're tired and outplayed.

The world's atoms are all drunk with love
drowned between negation and affirmation.

In the place where the sun casts its light
there's neither life nor death for the atoms.

What's your final word then, 'Aṭṭār?
Who knows this mystery and these allusions?

7

عشق جانان همچو شمعم از قدم تا سر بسوخت
مرغ جانرا نیزچون پروانه بال و پر بسوخت
عشقش آتش بود کردم مجمرش ازدل چو عود
آتش سوزنده برهم عود و هم مجمر بسوخت
ز آتش رویش چو یك اخگر بصحرا اوفتاد
هردوعالمهمچوخاشاکی ازآن اخگر بسوخت
خواستم تا پیش جانان پیشکش جان آورم
پیش دستی کرد عشق وجانم اندر بر بسوخت
نیست از خشك وترم در دست جز خاکستری
کاتش غیرت درآمدخشك وتر یکسر بسوخت
دادم آن خاکستر آخر بر سر کویش بباد
برق استغنا بجست ازغیب وخاکستر بسوخت
گفتم اکنون ذرّه ای دیگر بمانم گفت باش
ذرّه دیگر چه باشد ذره‌ای دیگر بسوخت
چون رسید این جایگه عطّار نههست ونهنیست
کفر و ایمانش نماند ومؤمن و کافر بسوخت

7

Love of the Beloved burned me like a candle, head to foot.
        My soul-bird burned like a moth, wing and feather.

The fire of her love smoked my heart like aloes;
        then her fire consumed both the smoke and the aloes.

A coal from her face fell into the desert:
        both worlds burned like kindling from her ember.

I was to offer my soul to the soul-mate.
        The Beloved outsmarted me; I got burnt.

There's nothing left of my blood or flesh, but ash;
        the zealous fire burned me altogether.

When I scattered the ashes upon her street
        the blaze of disdain struck and charred the remains.

So I said: *I've been reduced to particles.*
        She said: *That may be, but all particles shall burn.*

In ʿAṭṭār's state of neither being nor not being,
        neither doubt nor trust, the pious and the infidel both burn.

8

این چه‌سوداست کز تودرسرماست
وین‌چه غوغاست کز تو دربرماست

از تو در ما فتاده شور و شری
این همه شور و شر نه درخور ماست

تا تو کردی بسوی ما نظری
ملك هر دو جهان مسخّر ماست

پاکباز آمدیم از دو جهان
کاتشت در میان جوهر ماست

آتشی کز تو در نهاد دلست
تا ابد رهنمای و رهبر ماست

دیده‌ای کو که روی تو بیند
دیده تیره است ویار دربر ماست

ما درین ره حجاب خویشتنیم
ور نه روی تودر برابر ماست

تا که عطّار عاشق غم تست
دل اصحاب ذوق غمخور ماست

8

What's this sadness you've put in my mind,
and what's this madness you've instilled in me?

You've caused me much passion and mayhem;
but all this excitement doesn't suit me!

As soon as you pay me any attention
you make a world conqueror subject to me.

I've been cleansed of both worlds' influence
since your purging fire burns within me.

The fire that you've put in my heart's fabric
will eternally sustain and lead me.

Where's the observer to see your face?
Eyes are dim. The Beloved sees through me.

I've been shrouded by myself, or else
I'd see that your face is on a par with me.

For how long will 'Aṭṭār be grief's lover?
His experienced heart wants to grieve for me.

9

ترا در ره خراباتی خرابست — گر آنجاخانه‌ای گیری صوابست
بگیر آن خانه تا ظاهر به بینی — که خلق عالم و عالم سرابست
درآن خانه ترا یکسان نماید — جهانی گرپر آتش گر پر آبست
خراباتیست بیرون از دو عالم — دو عالم در بر آن همچو خوابست
ببین کز بوی دُرد آن خرابات — فلك را روز و شب چندین شتابست
بآسانی نیابی سرّ این کار — که کاری سخت و سرّی تنك‌یابست
بعقل این راه مسپر کاندرین راه — جهانی عقل چون خر در خلابست
مثال تو درین کنج خرابات — مثال سایه‌ای در آفتابست
چگونه شرح آن گویم که جانم — زعشق این سخن مست وخرابست
اگر پرسی ز سرّ این سؤالی — چگویم من که خاموشی جوابست
برای جست و جوی این حقیقت — هزاران حلق در دام طنابست
ز درد این سخن پیران ره‌را — محاسنها بخون دل خضابست
جوانمردان دین را زین مصیبت — جگرها تشنه و دلها کبابست
زشرح این سخن وز خجلت خویش — دل عطّار در صد اضطرابست

9

You've got drunk on the way to the tavern.
        You'd do well to find yourself a house there.

Seize that house, so you may see more clearly
        that the world and its creatures are a mirage.

In that house it won't matter to you
        if the world is consumed by flames or by water.

There is a tavern outside both worlds;
        the two worlds are asleep in its embrace.

See how the smell of the tavern's wine
        tempts the skies to rush through night and day.

Getting to the heart of the matter is hard;
        it's a tough matter, and has an illusive heart.

Don't let Reason be your guide on this road.
        This world's reason is an ass in the mire.

In the corner of the tavern you are
        like a shadow in the presence of the sun.

How can I recount this tale, when my soul
        is intoxicated and ruined by love?

If you ask me the secret of this question
        what can I say, for silence is the answer.

In seeking and finding this reality
        thousands of necks are put at the rope's mercy.

The pain of this truth has turned the beards
        of the journey's elders red with their hearts' blood.

Due to these ordeals, the young men of faith
have parched livers and char-grilled hearts.

Having told this tale in spite of himself,
ʿAṭṭār's heart is wildly excited.

10

عقل مست لعل جان افزای تست　　دل غلام نرگس رعنای تست
نیکویی را در همه روی زمین　　گرقبایی هست بر بالای تست
چون کسی را نیست حسن روی تو　　سیر مهر و مه بحسن رای تست
نور ذرّه ذرّه بخش هر دو کون　　آفتاب طلعت زیبای تست
درجهان هر جا که هست آرایشی　　پرتو از روی جهان آرای تست
تارخت شد ملك بخش هر دو کون　　مالك‌الملك جهان مولای تست
خون اگر در آهوی چین مشك‌شد　　هم زچین زلف عنبر سای تست
گر چه آب خضر جام جم بشد　　تشنهٔ جام جهان افزای تست
خلق عالم در رهت سر باختند　　ورکسی را هست سر همپای تست
آسمان سربر زمین هر جای تو　　در طواف عشق یك یك جای تست
آفتاب بی سر و بن ذرّه وار　　این چنین سرگشته در سودای تست
این جهان‌وآن‌جهان وهرچه هست　　شبنمی لب تشنه از دریای تست
چون بجز تو در دو عالم نیست کس　　در دو عالم کیست کو همتای تست
هرکرا هر ذرّه‌ای چشمی شود　　هم گر انصافست نابینای تست
گر فریدامروزچون شوریده‌ایست　　عاقل خلقست چون شیدای تست

10

Brain is drunk with your lush ruby lips;
heart is the slave of your fine narcissus.

It'd be fortuitous and pleasant to find
a tunic worthy of your figure in this world.

Because none can resemble your image
the path of the sun and the moon mimics you.

Bit by bit spreads across the universe
light from your beautiful face's sunshine.

If there is any beauty in this world
it's a ray of your beautifying glow.

Since your grace has granted us both worlds
the earth's greatest ruler is your priest.

If a Chinese deer's blood turns to musk
China's amber-scented curls are yours.

Even if Khiḍr's water fills Jamshīd's cup
he'll be thirsty for your world-displaying cup.

People have lost their heads on your path.
Those left alive do the same for you.

You have placed the skies above the earth.
You have placed us along Love's orbit.

The sun is like a frenetic particle,
hovering, baffled and besotted by you.

This world, the afterlife, and everything else
is a dew on lips longing for your ocean.

Since there's no one in either world but you
    who is there in either world to equal you?

Every element that gains vision
    will turn blind to do justice to you.

If Farīd is like a madman today
    he's sane among men but maddened by you.

II

چون کنم معشوق عیّار آمدست
دشنه در کف سوی بازار آمدست

دشنهٔ او تشنهٔ خون دلست
لاجرم خونریز وخونخوار آمدست

همچنان کان پسته می‌ریزد شکر
همچنان آن دشنه‌خونبار آمدست

هست ترك و من بجان هندوی او
لا جرم با تیغ در کار آمدست

صبحدم هر روز با کرباس و تیغ
پیش تیغ او بزنهار آمدست

آینه بر روی خود می داشتست
تا بخود بر عاشق زار آمدست

از وصال او کسی کی بر خورد
کو بعشق خود گرفتار آمدست

او ز جمله فارغست و هر کسی
اندرین دعوی پدیدار آمدست

لیك چون تو بنگری درراه‌عشق
قسم هر کس محض پندار آمدست

عاشق او و عشق او معشوقه اوست
کیستی تو چون همه یار آمدست

جز فنائی نیست چون می بنگرم
آنچه از وی قسم عطّار آمدست

11

I have a brigand of a Beloved.
  She's entering the bazaar with a dagger.

Her dagger is craving for heart's blood.
  She's come blood-hungry to shed my blood.

Like baklava pistachios that ooze sugar
  her dagger comes to us drenched in blood.

She's the Turk and I her devout Hindu;
  I'm accustomed to the deeds of her blade.

Every dawn, with scimitar and cloak
  we seek clemency beneath her sword.

She holds a mirror to herself so
  her self becomes her own jealous lover.

How is one to attain union with her
  while she's entangled in narcissistic desire?

She is removed from all, and all others
  appear demanding compared to her.

Yet you may see along the Path of Love
  each person's boon is mere opinion.

She is the Lover, Love, and the Beloved.
  Who are you then, when she's everything?

When I look there's only annihilation
  portioned to ʿAṭṭār by his Beloved.

12

زان پیش که بودها نبودست
بود تو ز ما جدا نبودست

چون بود تو بود بود ما بود
کی بود که بود ما نبودست

گر بود تو بود بود ما نی
موقوف تو بد چرا نبودست

ما بر در تو چو خاك بودیم
نه آب و نه گل هوا نبودست

در صدر محبّت نشاندیم
زان پیش که حرف لا نبودست

دریای تو جوش سر بر آورد
پر شد همه جا و جا نبودست

عطّار ضعیف را دل ریش
جز درد تو به دوا نبودست

12

Before anything came into being
    your being was not separate from me.

Since your being was the essence of my being
    when was it that my being could not be?

If your being hasn't been my being
    wouldn't my being be brought to an end?

I was the dirt at the feet of your door.
    Neither water nor clay aired through.

I sat upon the throne of your kindness
    where the word *lā* is never uttered.

Your sea was brought to boil and expanded;
    it filled every place, and 'place' was no more.

Feeble 'Aṭṭār is wounded in the heart.
    There's no remedy other than your pain.

13

آتش عشق تو در جان خوشترست — جان زعشقت آتش‌افشان خوشترست
هر که‌خورد از جام عشقت قطره‌ای — تا قیامت مست و حیران خوشترست
تا تو پیدا آمدی پنهان شدم — زانکه با معشوق پنهان خوشترست
درد عشق تو که جان می‌سوزدم — گرهمه زهرست از جان خوشترست
درد بر من ریز و درمانم مکن — زانکه درد تو ز درمان خوشترست
می نسازی تا نمی‌سوزی مرا — سوختن در عشق تو زان خوشترست
چون‌وصالت هیچکس‌را روی نیست — روی در دیوار هجران خوشترست
خشك سال وصل تو بینم مدام — لاجرم در دیده طوفان خوشترست
همچو شمعی در فراقت هر شبی — تا سحر عطّار گریان خوشترست

13

The fire of your love in the soul is sweeter.
    The life enflamed by your love is sweeter.

For those who had a drop from your love's cup
    drunkenness till the Judgement Day is sweeter.

I was hidden until you emerged,
    since being hidden with the Beloved is sweeter.

Even if your love's pain that burns the soul
    is all poison, it is sweeter than life.

Pour out pain for me and don't offer a cure
    since your pain is sweeter than any cure.

Don't build me up until you've burned me down;
    burning for your love is sweeter than that.

Since no one can reach union with you
    reaching the wall of parting is sweeter.

I foresee a lasting drought in our bond;
    no doubt foreseeing a flood would be sweeter.

In your absence, every night like a candle
    ʿAṭṭār's weeping till dawn is sweeter.

14

دوش ناگه آمد و درجان نشست — خانه‌ویران کردودرپیشان نشست
عالمی بر منظر معمور بود — او چرا درخانهٔ ویران نشست
گنج در جای‌خراب اولیترست — گنج بوداودرخرابی زان نشست
هیچ یوسف دیده‌ای کز تخت وتاج — چون دلش بگرفت در زندان نشست
گرچه پیدا برد دل از دست من — آمد و بر جان من پنهان نشست
چون مراتنها بدید آن ماه روی — گفت تنها بیش ازین نتوان نشست
جان بده وانگه نشست ما طلب — که توان باجان برجانان نشست
ازسرجان چون تو برخیزی تمام — من کنم آن‌ساعتت درجان نشست
چون‌زجانان‌این‌سخن‌بشنید جان — خویش‌رادرباخت‌وسرگردان نشست
خویشتن راخویشتن آن وقت دید — کوچو گویی درخم‌چوگان نشست
دایماً در نیستی سرگشته بود — زان چنین‌عطّار زان‌حیران نشست

14

Last night she suddenly came and seized my life.
    She destroyed the house and sat by the facade.

In a world that appears so prosperous
    why does she settle in a ruined house?

The riches in the ruins are most precious.
    She was the riches, and so stayed in the ruins.

Have you ever seen a Joseph who, grown
    weary of being king, stays in the prison?

Although she seemed to have stolen my heart
    she's secretly come to dwell in my life.

When the beautiful one found me alone
    she said: *No one can sit alone anymore.*

First, give up your life and seek us.
    Who expects the Beloved while clutching life?

When you've completely left your life
    at once I'll come to reside in your soul.

When my soul heard this from the Beloved
    it offered itself up and sat bewildered.

In that moment my self beheld itself
    like a ball in the curve of a polo mallet.

Ever perplexed in non-being
    it remained astonished like ʿAṭṭār.

15

تا عشق تو در میان جانست
جان بر همه چیز کامرانست

یارب چه کسی که در دو عالم
کس قیمت عشق تو ندانست

عشقت بهمه جهان دریغست
زانست که از جهان نهانست

اندوه تو کوه بی‌قرارست
سودای تو بحر بی‌کرانست

شادیّ دل کسی که دایم
با درد غم تو شادمانست

با تو نفسی نشسته بودم
دیریست کم آرزوی آنست

گر دست دهد دمی وصالت
پیش از اجل آرزوی آنست

جانا چو تو از جهان فزونی
خود جان ز چه بستهٔ جهانست

بی صبر و قرار جان عطّار
بر بوی وصال جاودانست

15

While your love is in the midst of the soul
the soul is successful in all things.

O Lord, is there anyone in both worlds
who doesn't know the price of your love?

The entire world has been denied your love
because it has been concealed from the world.

Grief for you is a quaking mountain;
passion for you a shoreless ocean.

Contentment is for those who are endlessly
contented with the pain of grief for you.

I sat with you only for a moment;
too little, too late for my wishes.

If I am to arrive at our union
my wish is to get there before death.

O soul, how will you surpass this world
as long as to this world you're attached?

This impatient, restless soul of 'Aṭṭār's
lives eternally on the scent of union.

16

جهانی جان چو پروانه از آنست — که آن ترسا بچه شمع جهانست
بترسایی در افتادم که پیوست — مرا زنّار زلفش بر میانست
درآمد دوش آن ترسا بچه مست — مرا گفتا که دین من عیانست
درین دین گر بقا خواهی فنا شو — که گر سودی کنی آنجا زیانست
بدو گفتم نشانی ده ازین راه — مرا گفتا که این ره بی نشانست
ز پیدایی هویدا در هویداست — ز پنهانی نهان اندر نهانست
فنا اندر فنایست و عجب این — که اندر وی بقای جاودانست
چو پیدا و نهان دانستی این راه — یقین می‌دان که نه این و نه آنست
بدین ما درآ گر مرد کفری — که عاشق غیر این دین کفردانست
یقین می‌دان که کفر عاشقی را — بنا بر کافریّ جاودانست
اگر داری سر این پای درنه — بترک جان بگو چه جای جانست
وگرنه با سلامت رو که با تو — سخن گفتن ز دلق و طیلسانست
برو عطّار و تن زن زانکه این شرح — نه کار تست کار رهبرانست

16

The world of soul is like a moth because
  of that young Christian who is the world's candle.

I've become a Christian since I wear
  an infidel's girdle woven from her hair.

Last night she came intoxicated
  and told me: *My religion is plain to see.*

In this faith, if you seek life you must wither;
  your profit here equals loss there.

I told her: *Show me its direction.*
  She said: *It's directionless.*

In coherence, it's clear in its clarity.
  In obscurity, screened by secrecy.

It's nothing within nothingness. How strange
  that it possesses everlasting life!

Since you know this Path is clear and concealed
  be certain that it's neither this nor that.

Come to our faith if you're an infidel:
  for Lovers, other faiths mean infidelity.

Surely the infidelity of Love
  is based on an eternal unbelief.

If you have a longing for this, step forward.
  leave your life and say 'What's the place of life?'

Otherwise, go in peace. With you I've been
talking of the dervish habit and the sash.

Be quiet, ʿAṭṭār. This narrative is not
your business; it's a job for the vanguard.

17

عشق جمال جانان دریای آتشینست

گر عاشقی بسوزی زیرا که راه اینست

جایی که شمع رخشان ناگاه بر فروزند

پروانه چون نسوزد کش سوختن یقینست

گر سرّ عشق خواهی از کفر و دین گذر کن

کانجا که عشق آمد چه جای کفر ودینست

عاشق که در ره آید اندر مقام اوّل

چون‌سایه‌ای بخواری افتاده در زمینست

چون مدتی برآید سایه نماند اصلا

کز دور جایگاهی خورشید در کمینست

چندین هزار رهرو دعوی عشق کردند

برخاتم طریقت منصور چون نگینست

هر کس که دُرّ معنی زین بحر باز یابد

در ملك هر دو عالم جاوید نازنینست

کاری قویست عالی کاندر ره طریقت

بر هر هزار سالی یك مرد راه‌بینست

تو مرد ره چه دانی زیرا که مرد ره را

اوّل قدم درین ره بر چرخ هفتمینست

عطّار اندرین ره جایی فتاد کانجا

برتر زجسم‌وجانست بیرون‌زمهر و کینست

17

The love of her beauty is a sea of fire.
        If you're a lover you'll burn; such is the Path.

Where a bright candle's flame suddenly heaves
        won't the moth burn? Its burning is certain.

If you want love's secret leave unfaith and faith.
        What room is there for them in Love's entrance?

The lover who comes to the Path's first stage
        falls in frailty like a shadow upon the ground.

After a while nothing remains of the shadow
        because the sun lies in wait in a distant place.

Many thousands of travellers made pretence to Love.
        Manṣūr is like the gemstone on the seal of the Path.

Anyone who claims the pearl of truth from this sea
        is forever cherished in the courts of both worlds.

The task of this Path is extremely arduous;
        one person each millennium sees the Path through.

How will you know the Persons of the Path? for they
        first walk on this Path, then on the Seventh Heaven.

Along the Path 'Aṭṭār came upon a place
        higher than body and soul, outside of love and hate.

18

سخن عشق جز اشارت نیست | عشق دربند استعارت نیست
دل شناسد که چیست جوهر عشق | عقل را ذرّه‌ای بصارت نیست
در عبارت همی نگنجد عشق | عشق از عالم عبارت نیست
هر کرا دل ز عشق گشت خراب | بعدازآن هرگزش عمارت نیست
عشق بستان و خویشتن بفروش | که نکوتر ازین تجارت نیست
گر شود فوت لحظه‌ای بی‌عشق | هرگز آن لحظه‌را کفارت نیست
دل خود را ز گور نفس برآر | که دلت راجزاین زیارت نیست
تن خود را بخون دیده بشوی | که تنت راجزاین طهارت نیست
پرشدازدوست هردوکون ولیك | سوی او زهرهٔ اشارت نیست
دل شوریدگان چو غارت کرد | بانگك برزد که جای غارت نیست
تن دراین کار در ده ای عطّار | زانکه‌این کار ماحقارت نیست

18

The word of Love is nothing but allusion.
Love is not bound by poetic metaphors.

The heart recognises the jewel of Love.
Reason has no inkling of this insight.

Love doesn't reside in interpretation.
Love isn't of the world of explanations.

Whoever has had a heart ruined by Love
afterwards will never know reconstruction.

Take a loan of Love and sell yourself
for there is no trade fairer than this.

If one moment passes by without Love
that moment will never find redemption.

Retrieve your heart from the grave of your desire.
Your heart won't receive any other visits.

Wash your body with the blood of your eyes.
Your body shall have no other cleansing.

Both worlds are filled with the Friend, and yet
there's no indication of Her Venus.

As She plundered the hearts of Her devotees
a cry arose: *This isn't the place for pillage!*

Give up your body for this task O ʿAṭṭār
because our vocation bears no malice.

19

دل کمال از لعل میگون تو یافت　　جان‌حیات از نطق موزون تو یافت

گر زچشمت خسته‌ای آمد بتیر　　زنده شد چون دُرّ مکنون تو یافت

تا فسونت کرد چشم ساحرت　　جامه پر کژدم ز افسون تو یافت

سخت تر از سنگ نتوان آمدن　　لعل بین یعنی دلش خون تو یافت

تا فشاندی زلف و بگشادی دهن　　عقل‌خودرا مست و مجنون تو یافت

ملك کسری در سر زلف تو دید　　جام جم در لعل گلگون تو یافت

قاف تا قاف جهان یکسر بگشت　　کاف کفر از زلف‌چون نون تو یافت

جمله را صدباره فی‌الجمله بدید　　هیچش آمد هرچه بیرون تو یافت

تا دل عطّار عالم کم گرفت　　رونق از حسن درافزون تو یافت

19

The heart found perfection in your ruby wine lips;
the soul found vigour in your melodious speech.

If wounded by an arrow coming from your eyes
one's brought to life by finding your hidden pearl.

When the sorcerer's eyes set to enchant you
his garment was filled by the scorpions of your magic.

One couldn't find a thing harder than stone, but
it turned to ruby when its heart found your blood.

When you spread out your curls and opened your lips
reason found itself drunken; your love-fool.

Reason saw Khusraw's realm in the tips of your curls;
it found the world-displaying cup in your ruby wine lips.

It incessantly searched all over the world
to find the *kāf* of *kufr* from your curl-like *nūn.*

In brief, when one gazed on the All a hundred times,
all that was found outside of you became nothing.

Once ʿAṭṭār's heart thought nothing of the world
it found prosperity in your provocative beauty.

20

ای آفتاب طفلی در سایهٔ جمالت
شیر و شکر مزیده ازچشمهٔزلالت

هم هردو کون برقی‌ازآفتاب رویت
هم‌نه سپهرمرغی دردام‌زلف وخالت

بر باد داده دل را آوازهٔ فراقت
درخواب کرده‌جان راافسانهٔوصالت

عقلی که درحقیقت بیدار مطلق آمد
تا حشرمست خفته درخلوت خیالت

خورشیدکاسمانراسررزمه می‌گشاید
یك تار می‌نسنجد در رزمهٔ جمالت

ترك‌فلك که‌هست‌اودرهندوی تودایم
سرپا برهنه گردان در وادی کمالت

سیمرغ‌مطلقی‌توبر کوه‌قاف قربت
پرورده هردو گیتی درزیر پرّوبالت

صفّ قتال مردان‌صفهای مژه‌تست
صد قلب برشکسته درهرصف قتالت

عطّارشدچوموبی‌بی‌روی‌همچوروزت
تا بوکه راه یابد در زلف‌شب‌مثالت

20

O the sun, an infant in your beauty's shadow,
has tasted milk and sugar from your sparkling spring.

Both worlds are lit by the sunshine of your face;
the Nine Spheres a bird, snared by your curls and mole.

The heart gives the song of our parting to the wind.
In sleep the soul has the dream of our union.

Reason, wide-awake in the realm of reality,
drunkenly dozes, and dreams of you until Judgement.

The sun, which opens the songs of the sky's epic,
does not amount to one note of your epic beauty.

The Turk of the heavens, always your Hindu
wanders naked through the valley of your perfection.

You are the supreme *sī-murgh* perched on Mount Qāf;
fostering both worlds under your wings and pinions.

The rows of your eyelashes are hordes of murderers.
A hundred hearts have been smashed by your killers.

ʿAṭṭār has become a hair in the absence of your day-like face,
hoping to find a path in your night-like ringlets.

21

رطل گران ده صبوح زانکه رسیدست صبح
تا سر شب بشکند تیغ کشیدست صبح
روی نهفتست تیر روی نهادست مهر
پشت بدادست ماه هین که رسیدست صبح
بر سر زنگی شب همچو کلاهست ماه
بر در قفل سحر همچو کلیدست صبح
ای بت بربط نواز پردهٔ مستان بساز
کز رخ هندوی شب پرده دریدست صبح
صبح بر آمد زکوه وقت صبوحست خیز
کز جهت غافلان صور دمیدست صبح
سوخته گردد شرار کز نفس سوخته
گنبد فیروزه را فرق بریدست صبح
بوی خوش باد صبح مُشك دمد گوییا
کز دم آهوی چین مُشك مزیدست صبح
نی که ازآنست صبح مُشك فشان کز هوا
نافهٔ عطّار را بوی شنیدست صبح

21

Pour a cup of morning draught; the dawn has arrived.
It has drawn its sword to sever the head of night.

Mercury's face is hidden; the sun's face is shown.
The moon quickly turns its back; the dawn has arrived.

The moon is like a cap on the night's Negro head.
The dawn is like a key in the morning's padlock.

O celestial harpist, play the drunkards' tune;
for the dawn has torn the veil off the night's Hindu face.

The dawn's climbed the hills. Rise for the morning draught!
The morning has blown its trumpet towards the ignorant.

The spark has set fire to the burnt out embers.
The turquoise dome's forehead is split by the dawn.

The sweet scent of the dawn is musky as though
it has tasted the musk of a Chinese deer's tail.

But the dawn hasn't scattered musk because of this.
It has caught the scent of 'Aṭṭār's perfumed pouch.

22

هردل که ز خویشتن فنا گردد / شایستهٔ قرب پادشا گردد

هر گل که برنگ دل نشد اینجا / اندر گل خویش مبتلا گردد

امروز چو دل نشد جدا از گل / فردا نه‌ز یکدگر جدا گردد

خاك تن تو شود همه ذرّه / هر ذرّه کبوتر هوا گردد

ور در گل خویشتن بماند دل / از تنگی گور کی رها گردد

دل آینه ایست پشت او تیره / گر بزدایی بروی وا گردد

گل دل گردد چو پشت گردد رو / ظلمت چو رود همه ضیا گردد

هر گاه که پشت و روی یکسان شد / آن آینه غرق کبریا گردد

ممکن نبود که هیچ مخلوقی / گردید خدای یا خدا گردد

اما سخن درست آن باشد / کز ذات و صفات خود فنا گردد

هر گه که فنا شود ازین هردو / در عین یگانگی بقا گردد

حضرت بزبان حال می گوید / کس ما نشود ولی زما گردد

چیزی که شود چو بود کی باشد / کی نادایم چو دایما گردد

گر می‌خواهی که جان بیگانه / با این همه کار آشنا گردد

در سایهٔ پیر شو که نابینا / آن اولیتر که با عصا گردد

کاهی شو و کوه عجب برهم زن / تا پیر ترا چو کهربا گردد

ور این نکنی که گفت عطّارت / هر رنج که می بری هبا گردد

22

Every heart that annihilates its self
becomes worthy of the King's confidence.

The flower that doesn't assume the heart's hue
will be afflicted by its own muddy essence.

If the heart and the clay are attached today
won't they separate from each other tomorrow?

Your body's clay will all turn to atoms;
each atom will turn into a spirit bird.

If the heart remains in the clay of the self
how will it abandon the grave's confinement?

The heart is a mirror with a tarnished back.
If cleaned it will reveal its countenance.

Clay becomes heart just as back turns to face;
when darkness is gone all shall illuminate.

Every time that back and front integrate
the mirror immerses in magnificence.

It's not possible for any creature
to turn God-like or become the Creator.

But a truthful thing could be said
if the essence and quality of the self fade.

Every time one becomes annihilated from these two
he will subsist in the essence of Oneness.

The Presence in speaking of this state says:
A person does not become Us, but becomes of Us.

When will a thing turn into the Existent?
    When will the temporal become Eternal?

If you are searching for this unknown life
    make yourself acquainted with these tasks.

Sit in the shadow of a master, for the blind are
    better off with walking sticks.

Become a straw and upset the mountain
    as the master changes you like amber.

If you do not do as ʿAṭṭār has told you
    every sorrow you suffer will turn to dust.

23

بودی که ز خود نبود گردد — شایستهٔ وصل زود گردد
چوبی که فنا نگردد از خود — ممکن نبود که عود گردد
این کار شگرف در طریقت — بر بود تو و نبود گردد
هر گه که وجود تو عدم گشت — حالی عدمت وجود گردد
ای عاشق خویش وقت نامد — کابلیس تو با سجود گردد
دل در ره نفس باختی پاك — تا نفس تو جفت سود گردد
دل نفس شد و شگفتت آید — گر یك علوی جهود گردد
هر دم که بنفس می برآری — در دیدهٔ دل چو دود گردد
بی‌شك دل تو از آن چنان دود — کوری شود و کبود گردد
عطّار بگفت آنچه دانست — باقی همه بر شنود گردد

23

The being that nullifies its self
    becomes worthy of a prompt Union.

The wood that hasn't wiped out the self
    cannot possibly become incense.

This incredible business takes place
    on the Path of your being and non-being.

Every time your existence becomes nought
    at once your nothingness becomes being.

O lover of self, hasn't the time come
    for your Iblis to bow down in prayer?

You gambled your heart away in desire's path
    so that your desire would bring you profit.

The heart becomes desire and you're amazed
    by the celestial converting to earthly faiths.

Every breath you draw for the sake of desire
    becomes like smoke in the eyes of the heart.

Unquestionably such a smoke would turn
    your heart into a singed and sightless thing.

And so 'Aṭṭār has said all that he knows;
    the rest depends on those who would listen.

قد تو بآزادی بر سرو چمن خندد

خط تو بسر سبزی بر مُشك ختن خندد

تا یاد لبت نبود گلهای بهاری را

حقا که اگر هرگز یك گل زچمن خندد

از عکس تو چون دریا از موج بر آرد دم

یاقوت و گهر بارد بر دُر عَدن خندد

گر کشته شود عاشق از دشنهٔ خونریزت

در روی تو همچون گل از زیر کفن خندد

چه حیله نهم برهم چون لعل شکربارت

چندانکه کنم حیله بر حیلهٔ من خندد

تو همنفس صبحی زیرا که خدا داند

تا حقّهٔ پر دُرّت هرگز بدهن خندد

من همنفس شمعم زیرا که لب و چشمم

بر فرقت جان گرید بر گریهٔ تن خندد

عطّار چو دُر چیند از حقّهٔ پر دُرّت

در جنب چنان درّی بر دُر سخن خندد

24

Your figure freely laughs upon the cypress in the field;
the down on your cheeks mocks the musk of Cathay.

If the spring flowers retain no memory of your lips
the rose will never have the right to smile from the meadows.

The sea has subdued the waves by your reflection;
the rubies and jewels of your rain laugh at the pearl of Eden.

If a lover is killed by your bloodthirsty dagger
a rosy smile will be blooming for you beneath the shroud.

How can I deceive you? Your sugar dripping ruby lips
laugh at my deceptions no matter how cunning my plans.

You're the companion of the dawn since the Creator knows
your casket full of pearls has never beamed from a mouth.

I'm the companion of the candle since my lips and eyes
weep for the soul's parting and laugh at the body's tears.

Since ʿAṭṭār has been picking the pearls of your casket
in the presence of such a Pearl he laughs at the pearl of words.

25

صبح بر شب شتاب می‌آرد / شب سر اندر نقاب می‌آرد
گریهٔ شمع وقت خندهٔ صبح / مست را در عذاب می‌آرد
ساقیا آب لعل ده که دلم / ساعتی سر بآب می‌آرد
خیزو خون سیاوش آر که صبح / تیغ افراسیاب می‌آرد
خیز ای مطرب و بخوان غزلی / هین که زهره رباب می آود
صبحدم چون سماع گوش کنی / دیده راسخت خواب می‌آرد
مطرب ما رباب می‌سازد / ساقی ما شراب می‌آرد
همه اسباب عیش هست ولیك / مرگ تیغ ازقراب می‌آرد
عالمی عیش با اجل هیچست / این سخن را که تاب می‌آرد
ای دریغا که گر درنگ کنم / عمر برمن شتاب می‌آرد
در غم مرگ بی نمك عطّار / از دل خود کباب می‌آرد

25

The morning rushes at the night.
        The night pulls a mask over its head.

The candle weeps at the dawn's smile
        and brings torment to the drunkard.

O wine-bringer, bring the ruby water;
        water my heart for one more hour.

Arise and pour Siyāwush's blood
        since the morning's come with Afrāsiyāb's sword.

Arise O minstrel; recite a ghazal!
        See how Venus is bringing a rebeck.

Listening to the songs in the dawn
        hardly brings any sleep to the eyes.

Our minstrel is playing the rebeck,
        our wine-bringer brings the wine.

Our pleasure is prepared for; yet
        death draws its sword from the sheath.

A world of pleasure is nothing
        if death's light is cast upon these words.

O alas! For if I hesitate
        existence goes rushing past me.

Dull 'Aṭṭār, grieving over death
        turns his heart into a shish-kebab!

26

چون شراب عشق در دل کار کرد — دل ز مستی بیخودی بسیار کرد
شورشی انـدر نهـاد دل فتاد — دل در آن شورش هوای یار کرد
جـامهٔ دریوزه بـر آتش نهاد — خرقهٔ پیروزه را زنّار کرد
هم ز فقر خویشتن بیزار شد — هم ز زهد خویش استغفار کرد
نیکوییهائی که دراسلام یافت — بر سر جمع مغان ایثار کرد
ازپی یك قطره دردِ درد دوست — روی انـدر گوشهٔ خمّار کرد
چون ببست ازهردوعالم‌دیده را — در میـان بیخودی دیدار کرد
هستی خود زیرپای آورد پست — وز بلندی دست در اسرار کرد
آنچه یافت ازیاری عطّار یافت — و آنچه کرد از همت عطّار کرد

26

As the wine of Love takes effect in the heart
the heart abandons itself in drunkenness.

The disturbance that befell the heart's core
desires for the Beloved amid this revolt.

It's hurled the beggar's garment into fire
and turned the azure cloak into infidel's belt.

It is sickened by its own poverty
and revokes its own vow of abstinence.

The goodness of Islam is sacrificed
at the convocation of the Magi.

In search of a drop of the Beloved's lees
it's heading for drunken seclusion.

As it tore its eyes away from both worlds
it began to see within selflessness.

It climbed over its own existence and
its hands reached the mysteries from that height.

Whatever 'Aṭṭār's found, he's found through intimacy;
whatever he's done, he's done in high hope.

عشق تو مست جاودانم کرد   ناکس جملهٔ جهانم کرد

گرسبك دل شوم عجب نبود   که می عشق سرگرانم کرد

چون هویدا شد آفتاب رخت   راست چون‌سایه‌ای نهانم کرد

چون‌نشان‌جویم ازتو در ره تو   کـه غم عشق بی‌نشانم کرد

شیرعشقت بخشم پنجه گشاد   پس بصد روی امتحانم کرد

دُردیم داد و درد من بفـزود   دل من بـرد وقصد جانم کرد

گفت‌ای‌دلشده‌چه خواهی کرد   گفتمش من کیم چه دانم کرد

تا ز پیشم چو آفتاب برفت   همچو سایه ز پس دوانم کرد

سایه هرگز در آفتاب رسد   آه کین کار چون توانم کرد

چند گویی نگه کن ای عطّار   که یقینها همه گمانم کرد

27

Your love made me eternally drunk;
    it made me a nobody throughout the world.

No wonder my heart's become weightless
    since the wine of Love weighs on my head.

Since the sunshine of your face appeared
    I have been shrouded truly like a shadow.

How can I search your clues along your Path
    since the sadness of Love has made me clueless?

The lion of your Love lashed its claws in anger,
    then tested me with a hundred gestures.

She gave me wine-dregs and my pain grew;
    she stole my heart and aimed at my soul.

She said: *O love fool, what will you do?*
    I told her: *Who am I to know what to do?*

When she abandoned me like the sunset
    I was made to run after her like a shadow.

A shadow shall never reach within the sun.
    Ah! How am I capable of doing this?

How much you talk! Look here, 'Aṭṭār;
    all the certainties have made me doubtful.

28

چون بـاد صبا سوی چمـن تاختن آورد
گـویـی بغنیمت همه مشك ختن آورد
زان تاختنش یوسف دل گر نشد افگار
پس از چه‌سبب غرقه بخون پیرهن آورد
اشکـال بدایع همه در پردهٔ رشکند
زین شکل که از پرده برون یاسمن آورد
هـر گز ز گل و مشك نیفتـاد بصحرا
زین بوی که از نافه بصحرا سمن آورد
صد بیضهٔ عنـبر نخرد کس بجوی نیز
زین رسم که‌در بـاغ کنون نسترن آورد
هـر لحظه صبا از پی صد راز نهـانی
از مشك بر افکند و بگوش چمن آورد
آن راز بطفلـی همـه عیسی صفتانرا
در مهد چو عیسی بشکر در سخن آورد
چون کرد گـل سرخ عرق از رخ یارم
آبی چو گلابش ز صفا در دهـن آورد
لاله چو شهیدان همه آغشته بخون شد
سر از غم کم عمری خود در کفن آورد
اول نفس از مشك چو عطّـار همی زد
آخر جگری سوخته دل‌تر ز من آورد

28

As the gentle wind swept over the grassland
you'd think it had raided all the musk of Cathay.

If its swiftness did not wound Joseph's heart
then why is it that his shirt is soaked in blood?

Unique forms all wear the veil of jealousy.
This form has brought jasmine from behind the veil.

Rose and musk will never reach the desert until
the scent of the deer has brought jasmine to the desert.

No one buys a hundred ambers with a barley grain
in the way narcissus has been brought to the garden.

Every time the breeze follows a hundred secrets
it takes musk and scatters it over the field's ears.

The secret's infancy has all the traits of Jesus;
like Jesus it speaks with sweetness from the cradle.

As the rose sweated from my Beloved's face
a pure moistener like rosewater entered my mouth.

The tulip is immersed in blood like the martyrs;
grief for a short life brings its head into the shroud.

At first 'Aṭṭār took a breath from the musk.
At last a scorched heart was moistened by grace.

29

زندهٔ عشق تو آب زندگانی کی خورد
عاشق رویت غم جان و جوانی کی خورد

هر که خورد از جام دولت دردردت قطره‌ای
تا که جان دارد شراب شادمانی کی خورد

جان چو باقی شد ز خورشید جمالت تا ابد
ذره‌ای اندوه این زندان فانی کی خورد

گر فصیح عالمی باشد به پیش عشق تو
تا نه لال آید زلال جاودانی کی خورد

دل که عشقت یافت بیرون آمد از بار دو کون
هر که سلطان شد قفای پاسبانی کی خورد

هر کسی گوید شرابی خورده‌ام از دست دوست
پادشه با هر گدایی دوستگانی کی خورد

جان ما چون نوش داروی یقین عشق خورد
با یقین عشق زهر بدگمانی کی خورد

چون دل عطار در عشقت غم صد جان نخورد
پس غم این تنگ جای استخوانی کی خورد

29

Whoever drinks the juice of life to live by your Love
can be your admirer and grieve for youth and life.

Whoever has a drop of bitter lees from your wealth's cup
will drink the wine of happiness for their days to come.

The one whose soul is an eternal garden by your sun
will feel a hint of grief in this transitory prison.

Whoever is erudite in your Love's company
must be muted or else know eternal muteness.

The heart that found your Love left the burden of both worlds.
Whoever becomes sultan is slapped on the neck by the guards.

Whoever says: *I've drunk wine from the Beloved's hand*
is the king who can make friends with any beggar.

Our soul drank Love's certainty like an antidote.
Who can be sure of Love yet poisoned by suspicion?

'Aṭṭār didn't feel the pain of a hundred lovelorn souls;
so he shall know only the misery of this refractory bone.

30

بوی زلف یار آمد یارم اینك می‌رسد
جان همی آساید و دلدارم اینك می‌رسد
اولین شب صبحدم بـا یارم اینك مـی‌دمد
وآخرین اندیشه وتیمارم اینك می‌رسد
در کنار جـوی‌باران قامت و رخسار او
سرو سیمین آن گل بی‌خارم اینك می‌رسد
ای‌بساغم کومرا خورد وغمم کس‌می‌نخورد
چون نباشم شادچون‌غمخوارم‌اینك‌می‌رسد
مدّتی تا بودم انـدر آرزوی یك نظر
لاجرم چندین نظر در کارم اینك می‌رسد
دین‌ودنیا ودل‌وجان[وجهان] ومال وملك
آنچه هست ازاندك وبسیارم اینك می‌رسد
روی تو ماهست ومه اندر سفر گردد مدام
همچو ماه از مشرق ره یارم اینك می‌رسد
بزم شادی از برای نُقـل سرمستان عشق
پسته و عنّاب شکّر بارم اینك می‌رسد
من باستقبال او جان بر کف از بهر نثار
یار می گـوید کنون عطّارم اینك میرسد

30

Here comes the scent of her curls; now my Friend arrives.
  Herein the soul is comforted; now my sweetheart arrives.

At first, the night; now the dawn appears with my Friend.
  At last, the reflection; and now my carer arrives.

On the banks of the streams, her face and her figure.
  Now the silvery cypress with the thornless rose arrives.

I'm so filled with sadness and no one feels sad for me.
  Hence I'm not to be happy until my consoler arrives.

For a while I was desirous of just one glance.
  No doubt many glances now smile upon my affairs.

Faith, world, life, universe, possession and property
  are all too little; and now my abundance arrives.

Your face is the moon and the moon constantly revolves.
  Like the moon from the east now my Beloved arrives.

A joyous feast of sweetmeats for those dead-drunk in Love.
  Now my bundle of pistachios and candies arrives.

When welcoming her I throw my life like confetti.
  My Beloved presently says: *Now my 'Aṭṭār arrives.*

پیر ما وقت سحر بیدار شد / از در مسجد برِ خمّار شد
از میان حلقهٔ مردان دین / در میان حلقهٔ زنّار شد
کوزهٔ دُردی بیك دم در کشید / نعره‌ای در بت و دُردی‌خوار شد
چون شراب عشق در وی کار کرد / از بد و نیك جهان بیزار شد
اوفتان خیزان چو مستان صبوح / جام می بر کف سوی بازار شد
غلغلی در اهل اسلام اوفتاد / کای عجب این پیر از کفّار شد
هر کسی میگفت کین خذلان چبود / کان چنان پیری چنین غدّار شد
هر که پندش داد بندش سخت کرد / در دل او پند خلقان خار شد
خلق را رحمت همی آمد بر او / گرد او نظّارگی بسیار شد
آنچنان پیر عزیز از یك شراب / پیش چشم اهل عالم خوار شد
پیر رسوا گشته مست افتاده بود / تا از آن مستی دمی هشیار شد
گفت اگر بدمستیی کردم رواست / جمله را می‌باید اندر کار شد
شاید ار در شهر بدمستی کند / هر که او پر دل شد و عیّار شد
خلق گفتند این گدایی کشتنیست / دعوی این مدّعی بسیار شد
پیر گفتا کار را باشید هین / کین گدای گبر دعوی‌دار شد
صد هزاران جان نثار روی آنك / جان صدّیقان برو ایثار شد
این بگفت و آتشین آهی بزد / وانگهی بر نردبانِ دار شد
از غریب و شهری و از مرد و زن / سنگ از هر سو برو انبار شد
پیر در معراج خود چون جان بداد / در حقیقت محرم اسرار شد
جاودان اندر حریم وصل دوست / از درخت عشق برخوردار شد
قصّهٔ آن پیر حلّاج این زمان / انشراح سینهٔ ابرار شد
در درون سینه و صحرای دل / قصّهٔ او رهبر عطّار شد

31

Our Master awoke at the crack of dawn.
He went from the mosque's door towards the tavern.

He went from the circle of the religious
to the midst of the circle of infidelity.

He drank up a flagon of lees in one gulp;
he shouted at an idol and became a wine-drinker.

As the wine of Love did its work on him
it made him loathed by the world's good and evil.

Falling and rising like a drunkard at dawn
he went to the bazaar clutching a cup of wine.

An uproar arose from the people of Islam:
How dare this Master become one of the infidels!

Everyone said: *Why such a desertion?*
Why would such a Master commit such treason?

Their reproach made his resolve stronger.
In his heart the people's reproach turned prickly.

The people had compassion on him
and he was surrounded by countless spectators.

With one drink such a beloved Master
was so disgraced in the eyes of the world's people.

The dishonoured Master was fallen drunk
until gaining a brief awareness from drunkenness.

He said: *If I've got drunk it's well and good.*
The whole of humanity must do the same thing.

Whoever is drunk in this city
gets to be courageous and reckless.

The people said: *This beggar is for killing!*
This heretic's presumptions are extreme!

The Master told them: *Do the deed quickly*
for this beggar declares he's a fire-worshipper.

Hundreds of thousands of lives are offered to Her,
for whom the souls of the righteous are sacrificed.

He said this and puffed out a burning sigh
while mounting the ladder towards the gallows.

Foreigners and citizens, women and men
hurled and heaped stones upon him from all directions.

The Master who gave up his life in his ascension
became intimate with the secrets of Reality.

Eternally sheltered by Union with the Friend
he has been nourished by the Tree of Love.

These days the story of Master Ḥallāj
brings happiness to the hearts of the pious.

Within the chest and the desert of the heart
his narrative has become the guide to 'Aṭṭār.

32

یک شرر از عین عشق دوش پدیدار شد
طای طریقت بتافت عقل نگونسار شد
مرغ دلم همچو باد گرد دوعالم بگشت
هرچه نه از عشق بود از همه بیزار شد
بر دل آنکس که تافت یک سر مو زین حدیث
صومعه بتخانه گشت خرقه چو زنّار شد
گر تف خورشید عشق یافته‌ای ذرّه شو
زود که خورشید عمر بر سر دیوار شد
ماه رخا هر که دید زلف تو کافر بماند
لیک هر آنکس که دید روی تو دین دار شد
دامِ سر زلف تو باد صبا حلقه کرد
جان خلایق چو مرغ جمله گرفتار شد
یک شکن از زلف تو وقت سحر کشف گشت
جان همه منکران واقف اسرار شد
باز چو زلف تو کرد بلعجبی آشکار
زاهد پشمینه پوش ساکن خمّار شد
هر که ز دین گشته بود چون رخ خوب تو دید
پای بدین در نهاد باز باقرار شد
وانکه مُقر گشته بود حجّت اسلام را
چون سر زلف تو دید با سر انکار شد
روی تو و موی تو کایت دینست و کفر
رهبر عطّار گشت ره‌زن عطّار شد

32

Last night a spark emerged from the eyes of Love;
it lit up the Path's opening; Reason was overturned.

The bird of my heart travelled both worlds like a wind;
it grew weary of anything that did not belong to Love.

The heart of those whose hair is twisted by this tale
prays to the idols and wears the infidel's girdle.

If you have found the warmth of the sunshine of Love
split quickly, for the sun of life is about to descend.

O moon face, whoever saw your curls remained faithless
yet those who saw your visage became believers.

The gentle wind swirled at the trap of your curls;
the souls of the creatures altogether captured like birds.

At dawn one ringlet of your mane was discovered;
the souls of the sceptics were all convinced of the secrets.

Again as your curls were wondrously revealed
the Sufi ascetics became residents at the tavern.

At seeing your fine face whoever had turned from faith
stood fast and became a confirmed believer again.

Whoever had been certain of Islam's ways
headed for agnosticism after seeing your curls.

Your face and hair are the signs of faith and faithlessness.
They guide ʿAṭṭār; and are the bandits along his Path.

33

برقع از خورشید رویش دور شد / ای عجب هر ذرّه‌ای صد حور شد
همچو خورشید از فروغ طلعتش / ذرّه ذرّه پای تا سر نور شد
جملهٔ روی زمین موسی گرفت / جملهٔ آفاق کوه طور شد
چون تجلّی اش بفرق که فتاد / طور با موسی بهم مهجور شد
قوّت خورشید نبود سایه را / لاجرم آن آمد این مقهور شد
قطره ای آوازهٔ دریا شنید / از طمع شوریده و مغرور شد
مدتی می رفت چون دریا بدید / محو گشت و تا ابد مستور شد
چون در آن دریا نه بد دید و نه نیک / نیک و بد آنجایگه معذور شد
هر دو عالم انگبین صرف بود / لاجرم چون خانهٔ زنبور شد
زانگبین چون آن همه زنبور خاست / هریکی هم زانگبین مخمور شد
قسم هریك زانگبین چندان رسید / کز خود و از هر دو عالم دور شد
سایه چون از ظلمت هستی برست / در بر خورشید نورالنّور شد
همچو این عطّار بس مشهور گشت / همچو آن حلاّج بس منصور شد

33

Veil retreats from the sunshine of her face.
Lo! Every atom's become a hundred houris.

Her bright face is like the sun that lights up
the universe bit by bit from tip to toe.

Moses gained the whole face of the earth;
all the horizons became Mt Sinai.

When revelation dawned upon the summit
Moses and Mt Sinai both became obsolete.

The sun's power doesn't cast a shadow.
Clearly when one arrives the other is vanquished.

A drop heard the melody of the sea
and grew frantic and vain out of greed.

It went on for a while. At reaching the sea
it vanished and was eternally concealed.

Since it saw neither good nor bad in the sea
there goodness and evil were both excused.

Both worlds used to be pure honey.
They've no doubt transformed into bees' hives.

When all the bees took off from the honey
every single one of them got honey-drunk.

Anyone who gained a portion of such honey
became distant from their self and from both worlds.

A shadow that escaped the darkness of being
became the Light of Lights in the sun's embrace.

This is how 'Aṭṭār has become so famous.
This is how Ḥallāj has become so victorious.

34

جهان از باد نوروزی جوان شد
زهی زیبا که این ساعت جهان شد

شمال صبحدم مشکین نفس گشت
صبای گرم رو عنبر فشان شد

تو گویی آب خضر و آب کوثر
ز هر سوی چمن جویی روان شد

چو گل در مهد آمد بلبل مست
به پیش مهد گل نعره زنان شد

کجایی ساقیا در ده شرابی
که عمرم رفت و دل خون گشت و جان شد

قفس بشکن کزین دام گلوگیر
اگر خواهی شدن اکنون توان شد

چه می جویی بنقد وقت خوش باش
چه میگوئی که این یك رفت و آن شد

یقین میدان که چون وقت اندر آید
ترا هم می بباید از میان شد

چو باز افتادی از ره ز سر گیر
که همره دور رفت و کاروان شد

بلایی ناگهان اندر پی ماست
دل عطّار ازین غم ناگهان شد

34

The world was renewed by the New Year's Day breeze
and was beautified at that hour. Splendid!

At dawn the northerly blew a musky breath
and the balmy breeze scattered ambergris.

It was as though Khiḍr's water and Kauthar's flow
streamed from all directions into the fields.

When the rose bloomed, the drunken nightingale
perched howling against the flower's cradle:

O Wine-bringer! Where are you? Give me wine
since my life's gone, my heart's hurt, my soul's finished.

To break out of this suffocating trap
desire must now become ability.

What do you seek? Make yourself happy now.
What do you mean *This is gone and that's finished?*

Be certain that when the time has come
you too shall be offered some wine.

If you have abandoned the Path, start again
since your comrade has long left with the caravan.

For the unexpected disaster along our Path
ʿAṭṭār's heart shall grow sad unexpectedly.

35

هر زمانم عشق ماهی در کشاکش می کشد
آتش سودای او جانـم در آتش می کشد
تـا دل مسکین من در آتش حسنش فتاد
گاه‌می‌سوزد چوعود و گه‌دمی‌خوش‌می کشد
شحنهٔ سودای او شوریدگان عشق را
هر نفس چون‌خونیان اندر کشاکش‌می کشد
عشق را با هفت چرخ وشش جهت‌آرام‌نیست
لاجرم نه‌بار هفت و نـی غم شش می کشد
جمع باید بود بر راهی چو موران روز وشب
هـر کرا دل سوی‌آن زلف مشوّش می کشد
خاطـر عطّار از نـور معـانی در سخن
آفتـاب تیر بـر چرخ منقّش می کشد

35

Every time Love pulls us down in the tug-of-war
    the flames of her passion draw us into the fire.

As my poor heart's fallen amid the blaze of her charm
    it either burns like aloes or breathes with pleasure.

With every breath the soldiers of her passion
    slaughter the admirers amid the massacre.

Love, restless with the Seven Wheels and the Six Ways,
    bears neither the Seven's burden nor the grief of the Six.

Assembled day and night like ants on the Path
    are all the bewildered whose hearts waft towards her curls.

From the spiritual light in words, 'Aṭṭār's mind
    draws the sun as an arrow over the painted sphere.

36

از می‌عشق نیستی هر که خروش می‌زند
عشق‌تو عقل‌وجانش‌راخانه فروش‌می‌زند
عاشق‌عشق‌توشدم‌ازدل وجان که عشق تو
پرده نهفته می‌درد زخم خموش می‌زند
دل چو ز دُرد درد تومست خراب می‌شود
عمر وداع میکند عقل خروش می‌زند
گرچه دل خراب من‌از می‌عشق مست‌شد
لیك صبوح وصل را نعره بهوش می‌زند
دل چوحریف درد شد ساقی‌اوست جان‌ما
دل‌می عشق‌می‌خورد جان‌دم نوش می‌زند
تا دل من بمفلسی‌ازهمه کون در گذشت
از همه کینه می کشد برهمه دوش‌می‌زند
تا ز شراب شوق‌تو دل بچشید جرعه‌ای
جملهٔ پند زاهدان از پس گوش می‌زند
ای دل خسته نیستی مرد مقام عاشقی
سیرشدی زخود مگرخون توجوش‌می‌زند
جان فرید از بلی مست می الست شد
شاید اگر ببوی او لاف سروش میزند

36

Whoever shouts for the wine of Love's oblivion
auctions their reason and being for your Love.

Since I fell in love with your Love, your Love has torn
the veil off my heart and soul, and wounded silently.

As the heart gets drunk and ruined on the wine of your pain
existence bids farewell and reason cries out.

Although my ruined heart got drunk on the wine of Love
the dawn of union beckoned sobriety.

The heart became the lees' rival, and our soul the wine-bringer;
the heart drinks the wine of Love and the soul praises the drink.

When destitution expelled my heart from the world
it bore the grudge of all and assaulted them all.

When the heart had a taste of the wine of your desire
all the ascetics' cautions were ignored by its ears.

O weary heart, you're not worthy of being a Lover
if you're content with yourself, if your blood doesn't simmer.

Farīd's soul said *Yes!* and got drunk on the wine of creation.
Maybe it's his perfume that makes the angels croon.

37

عشق را پیروجوان یکسان بود — نزداوسود وزیان یکسان بود
هم زیك رنگی جهان عشق را — نوبهار و مهرگان یکسان بود
زیر او بالا و بالا هست زیر — کش زمین و آسمان یکسان بود
بارگاه عشق همچون دایره‌ست — صدر او با آستان یکسان بود
یارا گر سوزد و گر سازد رواست — عاشقانرا این و آن یکسان بود
در طریق عاشقان خون ریختن — با حیات جاودان یکسان بود
سایه‌از کلدان که پیش آفتاب — آشکارا و نهان یکسان بود
کی بود دلدار چون دل ای فرید — باز کی با آشیان یکسان بود

37

In Love the old and the young are the same;
in Love's presence gain and loss are the same.

In Love the world is monochromatic;
in Love spring and autumn are the same.

The low is high and the high is low;
the earth and the heavens are the same.

The kingdom of Love is circular,
its throne and its entrance are the same.

The Beloved can either burn or build;
for the Lovers this and that are the same.

Along the Lovers' Path shedding blood
and everlasting life are the same.

Forgo all the shadows; before the sun
the visible and the hidden are the same.

Farīd, how is the Beloved like my heart?
How are the falcon and the nest the same?

38

هر کرا ذرّه‌ای وجود بود   پیش هر ذرّه در سجود بود

نه همه بُت ز سیم و زر باشد   کـه بت ره روان وجود بود

هر که یك ذرّه می کند اثبات   نفس او گبر یـا جهود بود

درحقیقت چو جمله یك بودست   پس همه بودهـا نبود بود

نقطهٔ آتشست در بـاطن   دود دیدن ازو چه سود بود

هر که آن نقطه دید هردوجهانش   محو گشته ز چشم زود بود

زانکه دو کـون پیش دیدهٔ دل   چون سرابی همه نمود بود

هر کـه یك ذرّه غیر می‌بیند   همچو کوری میـان دود بود

همچو عطار در فنا مـی‌سوز   تا دمی گر زنی چو عود بود

38

Whoever rests with one atom of existence
        kneels to worship each atom.

Not all idols are gold and silver;
        the traveller's idol is existence.

Whoever can justify one atom
        is Jewish or Zoroastrian in essence.

In fact since everything is the One
        every being is nonexistent.

The unconscious is the source of fire.
        What's to gain from watching the smoke?

In the eyes of those who see the source
        both worlds immediately disappear.

When the two worlds are seen with the heart's eyes
        they are like a mirage, devoid of substance.

Whoever sees an atom other than Hers
        is a blind person amid the haze.

If you applaud ʿAṭṭār while he burns
        he'll be like aloes in annihilation.

39

هر کرا ذوق دین پدید آید شهد دنیاش کی اذیذ آید

چه کنی در زمانه‌ای که درو پیر چون طفل نارسید آید

آنچنان‌عقل‌را چه‌خواهی کرد که نگونسار یـك نبید آید

عقل بفروش وجمله حیرت‌خر که ترا سود ازین خرید‌آید

این نه‌آن‌عالمیست ای غـافل که درو هیچکس پدیـد آید

نشود باز این چنین قفلی گر دو عالم پر از کلید آید

گر درآیند ذرّه ذرّه ببانگ آن همه بانگ ناشنید آید

چه شود بیش و کم ازین دریا خواجه گرپاك و گرپلید‌آید

هر که دنیا خرید ای عطّـار خر بود کـز پی خوید آید

39

How can a person with a taste for faith
have an appetite for the world's honey?

What can one do in an age when
a master is immature as a child?

What can be expected of a mind
that gets tipsy on one drink of wine?

Sell reason and bulk-purchase confusion;
you'll benefit from this acquisition.

This is not that world, O ignorant one,
in which not a soul can be made visible.

Such a padlock cannot be opened
even if both worlds were bursting with keys.

Even if every atom was to shout
all the commotion would go unheard.

What does it matter to this ocean
if a man dives in filthy or clean?

O 'Aṭṭār, whoever buys into this world
is an ass after an unripe ear of corn.

40

آن ماه برای کس نمی‌آید کو باغم خویش بس نمی‌آید

در آینه روی خویش می‌بیند در دام هوای کس نمی‌آید

گر تو بهوس جمال او خواهی او در طلب و هوس نمی‌آید

جانا ره عشق چون تو معشوقی در زیـر تك فرس نمی‌آید

در وادی بی نهـایت عشقش سیمرغ بیك مگس نمی‌آید

هرگز نشوی تو هم نفس کس را کانجا که تویی نفس نمی‌آید

خورشید بلند را چه کم بیشی کش سایه ز پیش و پس نمی‌آید

چون در قعرست «در» وصل تو جز بر سر آب خس نمی‌آید

در پای فراق تـو شوم پامال چون وصل تو دسترس نمی‌آید

عطّار کـه چینهٔ تـو می‌چیند مرغیست کـه در قفس نمی‌آید

40

That moon will not shine upon those
who haven't had enough of their sorrow.

Those who see their own face in a mirror
aren't snared by the desire for another.

If you have a craving for her face
she won't come to your whim and search.

O soul, if you're a Lover you won't
travel the Path like a galloping horse.

In the infinite valley of her Love
the *sī-murgh* will not fall for a fly.

You shall never find a soul-mate
because souls cannot enter your place.

What's no more or less than the high sun
will shadow neither before nor after.

Since the pearl of your union is deep
only seaweed comes up to the surface.

I've been trampled beneath your absence
since union with you isn't within my grasp.

'Aṭṭār, who gathers your snare of grain,
is a bird who cannot enter the cage.

41

دلم دردی که دارد با که گوید   گنه خود کرد تاوان از که جوید

دریغا نیست همدردی موافق   که بر بخت بدم خوش خوش بموید

مرا گفتی که ترك ما بگفتی   بترك زندگانی کس بگوید

کسی کز خوان وصلت سیر نبود   چرا باید که دست از تو بشوید

ز صد بارو دلم روی تو بیند   ز صد فرسنگ بوی تو ببوید

گل وصلت فراموشم نگردد   وگر خار از سر گورم بروید

غم درد دل عطّار امروز   چه فرمایی بگوید یا نگوید

41

To whom can my heart speak of its pain?
    To whom can I repent, for I've sinned again?

Alas! Isn't there an affable companion
    who would weep for my rotten fortune?

When you spoke to me of abandonment
    you were a dying person describing death.

Why should one wash their hands of you when
    they're not full at the table of your union?

My heart sees your face through a hundred walls;
    it breathes your scent from a hundred leagues.

I shall not forget the rose of your union,
    otherwise thorn shall grow upon my grave.

Today the desolation of 'Aṭṭār's heart
    speaks or shuts up according to your mandate.

42

ای در درون جانم وجان از تو بی‌خبر
وز تو جهان پُرست وجهان از تو بی‌خبر

چون پی برد بتو دل وجانم که جاودان
در جان ودر دلی دل وجان از تو بی‌خبر

ای عقل پیر و بخت جوان گرد راه تو
پیر از تو بی‌نشان وجوان از تو بی‌خبر

نقش تو در خیال وخیال از تو بی‌نصیب
نام تو بر زبان و زبان از تو بی‌خبر

از تو خبر بنام و نشانست خلق را
وآنگه همه بنام ونشان از تو بی‌خبر

جویندگان جوهر دریای کنه تو
در وادی یقین و گمان از تو بی‌خبر

چون بی‌خبر بود مگس از پرّ جبرئیل
از تو خبر دهند وچنان از تو بی‌خبر

شرح وبیان تو چه کنم زانکه تا ابد
شرح از تو عاجزست وبیان از تو بی‌خبر

عطّار اگر چه نعرهٔ عشق تو می‌زند
هستند جمله نعره‌زنان از تو بی‌خبر

42

You're within my soul and my soul receives no news of you;
You've filled the world but the world has no knowledge of you.

Understanding you immortalises the heart and soul.
You're within the heart and soul, but they have no knowledge of you.

Your Path seasons the reason and revives the fortune.
The seasoned can't find you; the youth have no knowledge of you.

Your image is on the mind and the mind is deprived.
Your name is on the tongue but the tongue has no knowledge of you.

All creatures are named and signified through your meaning;
these names and signifiers have no knowledge of you.

Those seeking treasures in your bottomless ocean,
both certain and doubtful, have no knowledge of you.

Since the fly is ignorant of Gabriel's flight
even your messenger has no knowledge of you.

What's to speak of or narrate, since you eternally
exhaust narration and grant speech no knowledge of you.

Even though 'Aṭṭār is shouting for your Love
none of the shouting crowd has any knowledge of you.

43

گر ز سرّ عشق او داری خبر   جان بده در عشق و در جانان نگر
چون کسی از عشق هرگز جان نبرد   گر تو هم از عاشقانی جان مبر
گر ز جان خویش سیری الصّلا   ور همی ترسی تو از جان الحذر
عشق دریاییست قعرش ناپدید   آب دریا آتش و موجش گهر
گوهرش اسرار و هر سرّی ازو   سالکی را سوی معنی راهبر
سرکشی از هر دو عالم همچو موی   گر سر مویی درین یابی خبر
دوش مست و خفته بودم نیمشب   کوفتاد آن ماه را بر من گذر
دید روی زرد ما در ماهتاب   کرد روی زرد ما از اشك تر
رحمش آمد شربت وصلم بداد   یافت یك یك موی من جانی دگر
گرچه مست افتاده بودم زان شراب   گشت یك یك موی بر من دیده ور
در رخ آن آفتاب هر دو کون   مست و لا یعقل همی کردم نظر
گرچه بود از عشق جانم پر سخن   یك نفس نامد زبانم کارگر
خفته و مستم گرفت آن ماه روی   لاجرم ماندم چنین بی خواب و خور
گاه می مُردم گهی می زیستم   در میان سوز چون شمع سحر
عاقبت بانگی بر آمد از دلم   موجها برخاست از خون جگر
چون از آن حالت گشادم چشم باز   نه ز جانان نام دیدم نه اثر
من ز درد و حسرت و شوق و طلب   می زدم چون مرغ بسمل بال و پر
هاتفی آواز داد از گوشه ای   کای ز دستت رفته مرغی معتبر
خاك بر دنبال او بایست کرد   تا نرفتی او ازین گُلخن بدر
تن فرو ده آب در هاون مکوب   در قفس تا کی کنی باد ای پسر
بی نیازی بین که اندر اصل هست   خواه مطرب باش و خواهی نوحه گر
این کمان هرگز ببازوی تو نیست   جان خود می سوز و حیران می نگر
ماندی ای عطّار در اول قدم   کی توانی برد این وادی بسر

43

If you know the mystery of Her Love
grant your soul to Love and behold the Beloved.

Since no one has ever survived Love
don't protect your life if you are a Lover.

If you've had enough of your life, bravo!
If you're worried and fearful for your life, beware!

Love is an ocean with concealed depth;
the ocean's water is fire, its waves treasures.

Its jewels are mysteries and each secret
the wayfarer's guidance towards meaning.

Grow out of both worlds like unruly hair
if you've received a whisker of this knowledge.

I was drunk last night and asleep by midnight
as that moon's attention shone upon my being.

She saw my frail face in the moonlight.
She saturated my listless face with tears.

She pitied me and granted me drink;
one by one my vines revived by the sherbet of union.

Although I fell drunk from that wine
one by one my hairs began to see.

Although I was drunk and brainless, I could
discern the two worlds in that sun's countenance.

Although my soul had much to say on Love
there was no air in my lungs to set off the tongue.

That moon-face tired and intoxicated me.
    She indeed abandoned me with no food and no rest.

Sometimes I would die; sometimes I would live;
    I'd burn like an early morning candle in between.

Finally a shout arose from my heart;
    waves arose from my heart's ocean of blood.

As I opened my eyes from that state
    I found no trace or sign of the Beloved.

Pain, remorse, passion and yearning
    brought my arms to flap like the wings of a dying bird.

A divine voice spoke from a hidden place:
    You, from whose grasp the precious bird has vanished!

One must become dust in Her wake,
    until you depart from this bathhouse by the door.

Yield. Don't beat water in the mortar.
    For how long do you plan to grow fat in your cage?

See that you're without need at your core,
    either you imagine yourself a minstrel or a mourner.

This bow was never meant for your arms.
    Your soul is burning and stares back dumbfounded.

You've remained at the first step, ʿAṭṭār.
    When are you able to traverse this valley to the end?

44

مست شدم تا بخرابات دوش   نعره‌زنان رقص کنان دُرد نوش
جوش دلم چون بسر خُم رسید   ز آتش جوش دلم آمد بجوش
پیر خرابات چو بانگم شنید   گفت درآی ای پسر خرقه‌پوش
گفتمش ای پیر چه دانی مرا   گفت ز خود هیچ مگو شو خموش
مذهب رندان خرابات گیر   خرقه و سجاده بیفکن ز دوش
کم زن و قلّاش و قلندر بباش   در صف اوباش بر آور خروش
صافی زهّاد بخواری بریز   دُردی عشّاق بشادی بنوش
صورت تشبیه برون بر ز چشم   پنبهٔ پندار بر آور ز گوش
تو تو نه‌ای چند نشینی بخود   پردهٔ تو بردر و باخود بکوش
قعر دلت عالم بی منتهاست   رخت سوی عالم دل بر بهوش
گوهر عطّار بصد جان بخر   چند بود پیش تو گوهر فروش

44

I got drunk at the tavern last night;
howling, dancing, drinking the wine-dregs.

As my heart's fervour topped the flagon
the fire of my heart brought it to the boil.

The Master of the tavern heard my noise
and said: *Enter, cloak-wearing boy!*

I told him: *Master, how do you know me?*
He said: *Don't speak of yourself. Be quiet.*

Take up the faith of the tavern's swindlers.
Throw off your cloak and your prayer-mat.

Become a gambler, a thug, a dervish;
yell out abuse among the hoodlums.

Shed the ascetics' purity with scorn;
drink the lovers' wine-dregs with pleasure.

Tear the mask of metaphors from your eyes;
take the cotton of reproach out of your ears.

You aren't you while you're at peace with yourself.
Rip down your veil and wrangle with yourself.

The depth of your heart is an endless world.
Face the direction of that world attentively.

Buy 'Aṭṭār's treasure for one hundred souls.
How much would you pay for it, jewel-seller?

45

عشق بالای کفر و دین دیدم　　بی‌نشان از شك و یقین دیدم

کفر و دین وشك و یقین گر هست　　همه با عقل همنشین دیدم

چون گذشتم ز عقل صد عالم　　چون بگویم که کفر و دین دیدم

هرچه هستند سدّ راه خودند　　سدّ اسکندری من این دیدم

فانی محض گرد تا برهی　　راه نزدیکتر همین دیدم

چون من اندر صفات افتادم　　چشم صورت صفات بین دیدم

هرصفت را که محو می کردم　　صفتی نیز در کمین دیدم

جان خود را چو از صفات گذشت　　غرق دریای آتشین دیدم

خرمن من چو سوخت زان دریا　　ماه و خورشید خوشه‌چین دیدم

گفتی آن بحر بی‌نهایت را　　جنّت عدن و حور عین دیدم

چون گذر کردم از چنان بحری　　رخش خورشید زیر زین دیدم

حلقه‌ای یافتم دو عالم را　　دل در آن حلقه چون نگین دیدم

آخرالامر زیر پردهٔ غیب　　روی آن ماه نازنین دیدم

آسمان را که حلقهٔ در اوست　　پیش او روی برزمین دیدم

بر رخ او که عکس اوست دو کون　　برقع از زلف عنبرین دیدم

نقشهای دو کون را زان زلف　　گره و تاب و بند و چین دیدم

هستی خویش پیش آن خورشید　　سایهٔ یار راستین دیدم

دامنش چون بدست بگرفتم　　دست او اندر آستین دیدم

هر که او سرّ این حدیث شناخت　　نقطهٔ دولتش قرین دیدم

جان عطّار را نخستین گام　　برتر از چرخ هفتمین دیدم

45

I saw Love above faith or infidelity;
I saw it bear no sign of doubt or certainty.

Faithlessness, assurance, doubt and religion
I saw convene in the presence of Reason.

Since I surpassed Reason by a hundred realms
I can say I discern infidelity and faith.

All the barriers along the Path are self-made.
I found them similar to Alexander's rampart.

You shall be fully effaced upon the Path.
I saw the road leading us closer to this.

When I took up the task of description
I saw the features with my bodily eyes.

For every feature I annihilated
I saw another one lying in ambush.

When my soul transcended description
I saw it drown in an ocean of flames.

As my harvest burned in that ocean
I saw the moon and the sun harvesting my crop.

You could say the ocean was infinite.
I saw the Paradise and the houris in it.

When I traversed such an ocean
I saw the Rakhsh of sun beneath a saddle.

I considered the two worlds as a ring;
I saw the heart as a gemstone upon that ring.

Finally when the veil disappeared
	I saw the face of my gorgeous moon.

Since the sky is the handle on her door
	I saw the earth bowing in front of her.

Upon her face, reflected in both worlds,
	I saw a mask of ambergris curls.

The plans for both worlds come from her locks.
	I saw them curled, knotted, brushed and bound.

Before that sun, one's entire existence
	is seen as a shadow of a truthful friend.

As I was hanging onto her skirt
	I saw her hands firmly in her sleeves.

Whoever realised the secret of this tale
	I saw the core of their life prosper.

I saw the first step for 'Aṭṭār's soul
	take him higher than the seventh Sphere.

46

ما ز خرابات عشق مست الست آمدیم
نام بلی چون بریم چون همه مست آمدیم
پیش ز ما جان ما خورد شراب الست
ما همه زان یك شراب مست الست آمدیم
خاكِ بدآدم كه دوست جرعه بدان خاك ریخت
ما همه زان جرعهٔ دوست بدست آمدیم
ساقی جام الست چون و سقیهم بگفت
ما ز پی نیستی عاشق هست آمدیم
دوست چهل بامداد در گِل ما داشت دست
تا چو گل از دست دوست دست بدست آمدیم
شست در افكند یار بر سر دریای عشق
تا ز پی چل صباح جمله بشست آمدیم
خیز و دلا مست شو ازمی قدسی از آنك
ما نه بدین تیره جای بهر نشست آمدیم
دوست چو جبّار بود هیچ شكستی نداشت
گفت شكست آورید ما بشكست آمدیم
گوهر عطّار یافت قدر و بلندی ز عشق
گر چه ز تأثیر جسم جوهر پست آمدیم

46

On the day of *Alast* we got drunk in the tavern of Love.
We spoke in the name of submission for we were all drunk.

In our company the soul drank the wine of *Alast*.
We all were companions in wine and got drunk on *Alast*.

Adam was dust as the Beloved poured a cup into his clay.
We all have ensued from the Beloved's chalice.

The bringer of the cup of *Alast* spoke when *He gives them to drink*:
In the Path of nonbeing we have fallen in love with being.

The Beloved had a hand in our clay for forty dawns
and we became kneaded clay courtesy of the Beloved's hands.

The Beloved cast a fishing-net upon the sea of Love
and after forty mornings we all were captured by the net.

Jump up, O heart! Get drunk on the celestial wine.
We haven't come to this tarnished place to sit down.

The Beloved is all-powerful, so there shall be no defeat.
She said: *Come shattered; we've come for the defeated.*

'Aṭṭār found a jewel in the lofty heights of Love,
but the material world's influence made it inferior.

47

عاشقی چیست ترك جان گفتن
سرّ کونین بی زبان گفتن

عشق پی بردن ازخودی رستن
علم پی کردن از عیان گفتن

رازهایی که در دل پرخونست
جمله ازچشم‌خون فشان گفتن

بزبانی که اشك‌خونین راست
قصّهٔ خود یکان یکان گفتن

همچو پروانه پیش‌آتش عشق
حال پیدای خود نهان گفتن

عاشق آنست کو چو پروانه
می تواند بترك جان گفتن

شیر چون می گریزد از آتش
شیر پروانه را توان گفتن

راه رو تا بکی بود سخنت
برتر از هفت آسمان گفتن

کم نه‌ای از قلم ازو آموز
ره سپردن سخن روان گفتن

کار کن زانکه بهترست ترا
کار کردن ز کاردان گفتن

جان بجانان خود ده‌ای عطّار
چنداز افسانهٔ جهان گفتن

47

What's being in Love? Abandoning life;
relating the worlds' secrets without tongue.

Grasping Love entails escaping from self;
learning knowledge, speaking with clarity.

The mysteries of the blood-filled heart
must be spoken through a bloodied vision.

With a tongue soaked in the blood of tears
one's tales must be recounted one by one.

Like a moth at the presence of Love's flame
manifestation speaks of its concealment.

The Lover is like the butterfly who
is willing to speak of departing life.

As the lion escapes from the fire
it reports on the moth's aptitude.

Travel the Path; for how can your words
be loftier than the Seven Heavens?

If you can't travel far learn from the pen;
assuming the Path entails fluent speech.

Take action; because it's better for you
to do than talk about knowing what to do.

Give your soul to the Beloved, 'Aṭṭār.
Why do you keep telling us fairytales?

48

گر مرد نام و ننگی از کوی ما گذر کن
ما ننگ خاص وعامیم از ننگ ما حذر کن
سر گشتگان عشقیم نه دل نه دین نه دنیا
گر راه‌بین راهی در حال ما نظر کن
تا کی نهفته داری در زیر دلق زنّار
تا کی ززرق ودعوی‌شو خلق را خبر کن
ای مدّعی زاهد غرّه بطاعت خود
گر سرّعشق خواهی دعوی ز سر بدر کن
در نفس سر نگون‌شو گر می‌شوی کنون‌شو
واز آب و گل برون‌شو درجان ودل‌سفر کن
جوهر شناس دین شو مرد ره یقین شو
بنیاد جان و دل را از عشق معتبر کن
از رهبر الهی عطّار یافت شاهی
پس گر تو مرد راهی تدبیر راهبر کن

48

Visit our quarter if you're infamous and disgraceful.
        Beware, for we're disgraced among the noble and the common.

We're mystified by Love; we have no heart, no faith, no world;
        look into our state if you're seeking a guide for the road.

For how long will you disguise your belt of infidelity?
        For how long will you spread the news of lies and hypocrisy?

You pretentious mystic, so satisfied with your own piety.
        Cast off your pretence if you yearn for Love's mystery.

Topple your base nature. If you must, do it this instant!
        Exit the water-and-clay; journey the soul and the heart.

Treat faith as a precious stone; become certain of the Path.
        Confirm that Love is the foundation of heart and existence.

By the divine leadership 'Aṭṭār found himself a king.
        If you're a person of the Path, progress with this leader.

49

گر مرد این حدیثی زنّار کفر بندی
دین از تو دوردورست برخویشتن چه خندی
از کفر تا گذشته دعوی دین مکن تو
گر محو کفر گردی بنیاد دین فکندی
اندر نهاد گبرت پنجه هزار دیوست
زنّار کفر تو خود گبری اگر نبندی
هر ذرّه‌ای ز عالم سدّیست در ره تو
از ذرّه ذرّه بگذر گر مرد هوشمندی
چون گویمت که‌خودرا می‌سوز چون‌سپندی
زیرا که چشم بد را تو در پی سپندی
مردانه پای درنه گر شیر مرد راهی
ورنه بگوشه‌ای رو گر مرد مستمندی
ای پست نفس مانده تا کی کنی تو دعوی
کافزون ز عالم آمد جان من از بلندی
هیچست هر دو عالم در جنب این حقیقت
آخر زهر دو عالم خود را ببین که چندی
عطّار مرد عشقی فانی شو از دو عالم
کز لنگر نهادت در بند تخته بندی

49

You're of our tradition if you've donned the belt of infidelity;
religion is far away from you and you're laughing at yourself.

If you haven't gone past infidelity, don't fake religion.
You can found faith if you've been razed by infidelity.

Fifty fiends lurk beneath your religious facade
if you don't assume the belt of infidelity.

Every bit of the world is an obstacle along your Path;
overcome them bit by bit if you are a clever person.

I recommend you to burn yourself like wild rue;
to the evil eye you always follow the wild rue.

Stride forth valiantly if you're the lion of the Path;
draw away and hide in a corner if you're afflicted.

O base nature, you only claim as long as you remain
unlike my soul that has risen above the world.

There's nothing in either world to compare with this truth.
You see your own worth when both worlds have ended.

'Aṭṭār, you're a man of Love; be wiped out from both worlds
so that you build a bridge upon the anchor of your spirit.

50

ای در میان جانم وز جان من نهانی

از جان نهان چرایی چون در میان جانی

هرگز دلم نیارد یاد از جهان و از جان

زیرا که تو دلم را هم جان و هم جهانی

چون شمع در غم تو می‌سوزم و تو فارغ

در من نگه کن آخر ای جان و زندگانی

با چون تو کس چو من خس هرگز چه سنجد آخر

از هیچ هیچ ناید ای جمله تو تو دانی

درخویش مانده‌ام من جان میدهم بخواهش

تا بو که یک زمانم از خود مرا ستانی

گفتی ز خود فنا شو تا محرم من آیی

بندیست سخت محکم این هم تو می‌توانی

عطّار راز عالم گم شد نشان بکلّی

تا چند جویم آخر از بی‌نشان نشانی

50

You who are inside my soul and hiding from my soul;
why do you hide from my soul when you're within my soul?

My heart will never remember life and the world
because you are both my heart's life and my heart's world.

I burn like a candle in grief for you, yet you're unmoved.
Look upon me at last, my life, my existence.

How could a rogue like me compare with nobility like you?
Naught comes from my nothing; you know you're everything.

I'm self-absorbed but yield my life upon your request
so that for once you might liberate me from my self.

You said: *Efface your self to become my intimate.*
You can bind me to this as tightly as you please.

'Aṭṭār lost all trace of the mysteries of the world.
When will this search for the enigma's clues end?

NOTES TO THE TRANSLATIONS

The Persian text used in this volume is that of Taqī Tafaḍḍulī (1967), with permission from the publishers (originally Tehran, Bungāhi Tarjama u Nashri Kitāb, but now Tehran, Sharka Intishārāt ʿIlmī u Farhangī). This edition (hereafter T) has a critical apparatus, with important manuscript readings, though these have been omitted in the texts copied above. T sometimes provides vocalisation in cases of ambiguous homographs, such as *dard/durd*, and the *tashdīd*. The stability of verse order, unlike the situation with editions of Ḥāfiẓ, allows the text of T to be read with confidence; there are some minor differences from Saʿīd Nafīsī's edition (1339 a.h.s., hereafter N).

1

[T1;N1]

The first *ghazal* in a *dīwān* is exemplary for the style and message of the poet; this is true for Ḥāfiẓ and Rūmī, as much as for ʿAṭṭār. The main themes of this poem include the lover/poet's unceasing anguish, and the contradictions of the two opposing 'paths' to knowledge or love of the divine.

v.1, 3 Wine dregs or lees: drinking deeply, a metaphor of direct mystical experience.

Following verse 4, N has an extra verse:

> Except for pain there is no remedy, there where pain is
> for some of her hidden veils became visible to us.

2

[T2]

Images of light and revelation dominate this *ghazal.*

v.1 Moses is a paradigmatic mystical figure because of his vision of God on Mt. Sinai (e.g. Qur. 7.142ff). See R.A. Nicholson (ed.) (1898; repr. 1977), *Selected Poems from the Dīvāni Shamsi Tabrīz*, Cambridge, Cambridge University Press, (hereafter: *DST*) 16.15: 'The light of the face of Moses son of ʿImrān is my desire'.

v.3 The 'manna and quails' (Qur. 2.57, etc.) alludes to God's provision for the Israelites in their desert wanderings.

v.7 Mānī is the 3rd century C.E. Persian founder of Manichaeism, a Gnostic, dualistic religious sect which influenced Christian beliefs considerably (St. Augustine of Hippo being a follower before his conversion). In Persian literature, Mānī is nearly always associated with painting, specifically with a mythical gallery of beautiful paintings; the illuminated manuscripts of the sect were probably the reason for this association (Annemarie Schimmel, *I am Wind, You are Fire: The Life and Work of Rumi,* Boston, Shambhala, 1996, p.111).

3

[T6;N6]

4

[T9;N7]

v.6 Compare Rūmī's verse (*DST* 4.7):

> 'Tis notorious that copper by alchemy becomes gold:
> Our copper has been transmuted by this rare alchemy'

5

[T15;N12]

This love poem shows ʿAṭṭār in a rare festive mood. The convivial banqueting scene is reminiscent of early courtly poetry, reaching back to pre-Islamic times (see E. Yarshater, 'The Theme of Wine-drinking and the Concept of the Beloved in Early Persian Poetry', *Studia Islamica,* no. 13, 1960, pp.43-53). The poet's more somber temperament, however, is never far below the surface, as shown in the last verse. The mystical intent of this poem, the experience of union with the Beloved in the sacred hours of darkness, is clearly expressed. There are echoes in Rūmī's later work, e.g. *DST* no. 38.

6

[T17; N14]

This narrative *ghazal* of the *qalandarī* genre is one of the best examples of its type in 'Aṭṭār's *Dīwān*.

v.1 Reading *ṭā'āt* 'obedience' with N instead of T's *ṭāmāt* 'incoherent speech'.

v.11 Freed from the Pharaoh of bodily existence, the 'poet' becomes like Moses encountering the divine presence at the appointed hour on Mt. Sinai. Already by the 8th century, a Sufi Qur'ān commentary attributed to Ja'far Ṣādiq (d. 765) has the 'appointed place' of Qur. 7.142 glossed as 'the seeking of vision', an early interpretation of Moses' revelation as a mystical encounter.

v.13 Cf. *DST* 26.2: 'His sun peeped forth from mine eye'.

v.17 All the world's atoms are drunk with the wine of pre-eternal love in the covenant of *Alast* (Qur. 7.172); Cf. Ibn al-Fāriḍ's (d. 1235) famous wine poem which begins:

'We drank upon the remembrance of the Beloved a wine wherewith we were drunken before ever the vine was created.' (A.J. Arberry, *Arabic Poetry: A Primer for Students*, Cambridge, Cambridge University Press, 1965, p. 126.).

All reality is held in tension between negation and affirmation, the mystic's experience of *fanā'* and *baqā'*, ultimately based on Qur. 55.26-7.

7

[T25; N17]

This *ghazal* deftly combines the theme of the Beloved's utter cruelty, a common subject of the love lyric, with a wealth of images concerning fire and burning. The binary categories of mainstream religion won't suffice for unitary consciousness: both believer and infidel are burned.

8

[T36; N36]

A fine example of 'Aṭṭār's pure and direct language, without excessive rhetorical display or hyperbole, yet with emotion barely contained.

9

[T40; N43]

The 'house' in the opening verses probably refers to the inner 'house' of the soul or heart. 'Seizing' or occupying that house and the vision of

Reality thus gained allows one to see the world more clearly for what it is, a mirage.
v.7 The image of reason as an ass stuck in a mire recurs in the opening discourse of Rūmī's *Mathnawī* (Book 1, line 115).
v.10 The answer to any question about the soul's secret is the imperative of silence, the same imperative made innumerable times by Rūmī in his *Dīwān*.

10

[T43; N49]
This is a fine example of the use of hyperbole. The attributes of the Beloved are described in such exaggerated fashion as to stretch metaphor beyond the point of reason. The divine Beloved is seen as utterly peerless and beyond comparison, though the rhetoric derives from earlier forms of panegyric poetry which praised kings and generous patrons.
v.7 The reddish brown colour of deer's musk suggests an association with blood.
v.8 Khiḍr is a shadowy figure in Muslim mythology. In the Qur'ān he is traditionally associated with the mysterious guide of Moses, performing apparently evil deeds to test Moses' patience and faith (Qur. 18.60-82). In poetry he is usually associated with immortality, with the water or fountain of eternal life. Jamshīd is a legendary Persian king featuring in Firdawsī's epic *Shāh-nāma* (*Book of Kings*). He is associated (as suggested by his name) with a magical cup or goblet (*jām*) which allowed him a vision of the whole world.
v.9 Cf. *DST* 2.3-4: 'When you see in the pathway a severed head which is rolling toward our field, ask of it, ask of it, the secrets of the heart'.

11

[T49; N56]
This poem combines two conventional themes: describing the Beloved's cruelty and praising Her beauty.
v.4 A classic juxtaposition of the contrasting pair: the lawless, cruel and beautiful Turk, and the dark slave Hindu. Annemarie Schimmel mentions that 'Hindu' in 'Aṭṭār's poetry nearly always refers to a mean but obedient servant ('Turk and Hindu: A Literary Symbol', *Acta Iranica*, no. 3, 1974, pp.243-8).

12

[T58; N58]

A poem of philosophical genre, the theme of this *ghazal* is the eternity and pre-existence of the divine Being, and as we learn from the first few verses, the eternity of all being. This pan-en-theistic view is in tension with the traditional doctrine of creation. This *ghazal* is notable for its brevity of expression, showing fine poetic craftsmanship in condensing difficult subject matter into such a compact form. ʿAṭṭār uses word plays and 'word-knots' involving the use of the verbal form *būd* 'was; being'. Thus in verse 2 *būd* is used no less than seven times in a verse of only thirteen words.

v.4 'water' and 'clay' is a hendiadys for the human body.

v.5 *lā* is the Arabic negative particle 'no'.

13

[T61; N61]

14

[T74; N69]

The Beloved's 'visit' to the 'soul' at night and holding a lovers' converse is a recurring theme in ʿAṭṭār's poetry. The night setting is significant as it represents the time of meditation, prayer and devotion, when mystical experience is awakened in the aware and prepared consciousness. The notion of a 'ruined house' or of the 'visitor' destroying the house of the soul before taking up residence is a familiar idea reflecting the purification of the self before mystical gnosis can be attained. (See Mir Valiuddin, *Contemplative Disciplines in Sufism*, London & The Hague, East-West Publications, 1980, chapter 1).

v.4 Cf. the story of Joseph in the Qur'ān, chapter 12.

v.7 'life' (or soul): *jān* , 'Beloved' (or Soul): *jānān*.

15

[T88; N79]

v.4 The 'quaking mountain' refers to Mt Sinai. When God revealed Himself to Moses, He made the mountain 'crumble to dust, and Moses fell in a swoon' (Qur. 7.143).

16

[T89; N80]
The image of the 'young Christian' is reminiscent of the rhetoric of wine *ghazals*, with a stock character being the beautiful young wine-bringer (*sāqī*) with whom the drinkers and the 'poet' become infatuated. Wine drinking was associated with non-Muslim faiths, partly because it was assumed that its illegality in Islam meant that it was abundant in other religions. It may also have been associated with Christianity because of the centrality of wine in the Eucharist, and also because early Christian monks in the Middle East described mystical awakening as intoxication. But the supposed 'Christian' faith outlined here has all the features of the Sufi path itself, complete with the twin concepts of *fanā'* and *baqā'* (see note on *ghazal* 6 above).
v.2 'infidel's girdle' or belt (*zunnār*) worn around the waist by people of non-Muslim faiths.
v.13 N reads: 'Be quiet, 'Aṭṭār, leave behind this attachment to words, for in this you have a hearer in the placeless.'

17

[T96; N91]
A love *ghazal* emphasizing the path (*ṭarīqa*) of the lover. It may be the mystic's path or progress through the structures and conventions of a Sufi order, but this is debatable given the rudimentary nature of the Sufi orders or brotherhoods in 'Aṭṭār's day. It is best to read this *ghazal* more literally, seeing the path of the lover toward the Beloved as a simple metaphor without the added symbolism of a 'path' within a structured Sufi order.
v.6 Manṣūr al-Ḥallāj is the controversial Sufi who was executed in 922. 'Aṭṭār had a high regard for him, and a special relationship with this central figure in Sufi history (see Farīd al-Dīn 'Aṭṭār, *Muslim Saints and Mystics*, trans. A.J. Arberry, London, Boston & Henley, Routledge & Kegan Paul, 1966).
v.9 Rūmī later wrote:

> This is Love: to fly heavenward,
> To rend, every instant, a hundred veils.
> The first moment, to renounce life;
> The last step, to fare without feet. (*DST*. 35.1-2).

18

[T110; N100]
Verse 1 epitomizes the nature of love imagery in poetry: speech about love is only an indication, sign or allusion (*ishāra*), nothing more; nor is love bound by the symbolism of metaphor or rhetoric.

19

[T 136; N130]
N omits verse 3.
v.6 Khusraw is a legendary king featuring in Firdawsī's *Book of Kings*. (See note to *ghazal* 10 v.8 above.)
v.7 The Arabic/Persian letters *kāf* and *nūn* allude to the divine creative fiat *kun* 'be!' from the Qur'ān (2.117, etc.). The letter *nūn* is almost a complete circle with a dot at the top in its isolate or final-letter form, hence the visual similarity with hair curls. The letter *kāf* is also the first letter of *kufr* 'infidelity'.

20

[T145; N136]
v.2 The Nine Spheres of medieval cosmology.
v.6 See note on *ghazal* 11 v.4 above.
v.7 The *sī-murgh* is a mythical bird favoured by Persian poets. It lives on Mt. Qāf, a legendary high mountain on the 'horizons' of the earth, and represents the divine King (see Annemarie Schimmel, *The Triumphal Sun: A Study of the Works of Jalāloddin Rumi*, London, East-West Publications, 1980, p.123). The *sī-murgh* was made famous in 'Aṭṭār's celebrated work, *The Conference of the Birds*, when the thirty birds who finished their journey of self discovery realised that they themselves were the 'supreme bird' of their quest, *sī murgh* meaning literally 'thirty birds'.

21

[T151; N143]
This ghazal celebrating the appearance of dawn shows that 'Aṭṭār is a gifted nature poet, contrary to the views of some that he lacked this quality (notably the inference in Jan Rypka, 'Poets and Prose Writers of the Late Saljuq and Mongol Periods', in *The Cambridge History of Iran*, vol. 5, J.A. Boyle (ed.), Cambridge, Cambridge University Press, 1968,

p.590). It is true that 'Aṭṭār does not engage in lengthy descriptions of nature, and he does not use natural imagery for its own sake, but seldom is a *ghazal* found without some reference to the natural world.
v.8 An excellent pun on the *takhalluṣ* (mention of the poet's name), with reference to the musk pouch belonging to the 'perfumer', the literal meaning of 'Aṭṭār.

22

[T176; N164]
A philosophical or didactic *ghazal* in which the poet stresses the importance of the heart being emptied of all ideas of 'self'.
v.2 A pun on the homographs *gul* 'flower' and *gil* 'mud/clay'.
v.9 The poet argues against the notion of *ḥulūl*, 'divine indwelling' or fusing of the mystic's spirit with the divine. This is perhaps a counter to Christian/Gnostic ideas associated with incarnation, and also argues against similar Sufi notions linked with controversial figures such as Ḥallāj and Bisṭāmī.
v.11 'annihilated from these two' i.e. from the duality of the mirror.
v.16 Linking *kāh* 'straw' and *kūh* 'mountain' is a favourite poetic pun, a figure of contrast between things small and great. Amber (*kāh-rubā* , literally 'straw attracting') is often added to this play on words.

23

[T177; N165]
This *ghazal* follows the previous one in both T and N, and continues the same themes.
v.4 The mystic's life remains (*baqā'*) in God after the annihilation (*fanā'*) of the self.
v.5 Iblis was the disobedient angel who refused to bow down to the newly created Adam (Qur. 2.34, etc.).
v.6-8 'desire' or 'base soul' (*nafs*).

24

[T181; N169]
The rhyme end-word 'laughs' allows for several references to the mouth and teeth ('pearls'/ 'gems'/ 'rubies'). In the last verse the poet uses the image of pearls to refer to a treasury of words or poetry, the assembled jewel-like verses of the *ghazal*.

25

[T185; N171]
N omits verses 4 and 5.
v.4 In Firdawsī's *Book of Kings* Siyāwush was a fugitive prince murdered by the archetypal enemy of Iran, Afrāsiyāb, king of Tūrān. Legend has it that a reddish coloured tree named 'Siyāwush's blood' grew in the place where he was killed (See the dictionary of Ibn Khalaf Tabrīzī, *Burhān-i Qāṭiʿ*, M. Muʿīn (ed.), Tehran, Amīr Kabīr, vol.2, 1982, p.796).

26

[T204; N186]
v.3 'beggar's garment', 'azure cloak' i.e. Sufi garb.
v.7 'selflessness' (*bī-khwudī*) means literally outside of one's senses, beyond one's self, or ec-static.

27

[T207; N190]

28

[T216; N201]
Another *ghazal* illustrating the poet's skilful use of natural imagery involving scents, tastes and flowers.
v.2 For Joseph's blood-stained shirt, see Qur'ān 12.18.
v.7 For Jesus' miraculous speech from the cradle, see Qur'ān 19.29ff.

29

[T224; N204]
v.8 'refractory bone', a symbol of the body.

30

[T242; N221]
A rare example of a *ghazal* expressing intimacy and joy experienced with the Beloved. Yet even in this fulfilment of the lover's quest, sadness (verse 4) is never absent.
v.3 A rare mention of a thornless rose.
v.8 Compare Rūmī's lines:

> What does a drunken man desire except sweetmeats and a cup of wine?
> Sweetmeats derived from the soul, a cup of the Absolute Light,
> An eternal banquet laid in the privacy of 'He is the Truth' (*DST* 40.2-3)

31

[T251; N233]

This remarkable *ghazal* is of the 'master-and-tavern' genre. The correlation of wine drinking with mystical experience and adopting infidel faith are linked, in stylized fashion, with the controversial career of the Sufi martyr Manṣūr al-Ḥallāj (d.922). It is clear from the final verses that ʿAṭṭār aligns his own 'path' with that of Ḥallāj. See further Kenneth Avery, 'The Theme of the Sufi Master and the Tavern in the Lyric Poetry of ʿAṭṭār', *Sufi*, no. 48, 2000/01, pp.8-13.

v.11 'awareness' (*hushyār*) is the sense of Sanskrit *buddha* 'awake, enlightened'.

32

[T253; N235]

v.1 'the Path's opening', literally the '*ṭ*' of *ṭarīqa* 'path'.

33

[T256; N236]

v.4 See Qur'ān 7.143.

v.13 'victorious' (*manṣūr*) is one of Ḥallāj's names.

34

[T263; N246]

v.3 'Khiḍr's water and Kauthar's flow' (Qur. 108.1), the 'water' of eternal life and paradise.

35

[T273; N 240]

v.4 The 'Seven Wheels' or spheres of the heavens contrast with the 'Six Ways' or dimensions of the earth, regarded as a cube.

36

[T310; N277]

v.9 The soul submitted to the divine will and drank 'wine' on the day of creation (*Alast*, Qur. 7.172), when all souls answered 'yes' to the lordship of God.

37

[T333; N305]

38

[T338; N297]
This *ghazal* expresses the uncompromising theosophy of monism, that since all real existence is the One, no other 'thing' exists (See Hellmut Ritter, *Das Meer der Seele: Mensch, Welt und Gott in den Geschichten des Farīduddīn 'Aṭṭār*, Leiden, E.J. Brill, 1978, pp.601ff.). The very idea of the existence of anything other than the One implies idol worship, since it is affirming something other than the divine unity.

39

[T359; N324]
v.1 'taste for faith' (*dhawq-i dīn*). *dhawq* 'taste' is direct, unmediated experience, a keyword of the Sufis.
v.7 Every atom praises God continually, yet their sound is unheard by any except God. Cf. Rūmī:

> 'I am silent. Speak, O soul of soul of soul,
> from desire of whose face every atom grew articulate.'
> (*DST* 1.18)

v.9 Some word plays: whoever buys (*kharīd*) into this world is an ass (*khar*) after an unripe ear of corn (*khawīd*).

40

[T370; N334]
v.5 See note on *ghazal* 20 v. 7 above.
v.8 Cf. Rūmī:

> 'Songs are spindrift on the face of the sea;
> no pearl comes on the surface of the sea.'

(Arberry, A.J., *Mystical Poems of Rūmī*, Chicago and London, University of Chicago Press, 1968, 13.6)
v.10 'snare' (*chīna*) also carries the meaning 'course of bricks or stones', and thus alludes to the poet who 'gathers' (*chīnad*) lines like courses of stone.

41

[T391; N352]

42

[T403; N366]
This *ghazal* speaks of the 'hidden treasure' of divine knowledge, the eternal

mystery of God's wisdom, hidden yet manifest in all Creation. The poem is based on the *ḥadīth* (sacred Tradition): 'I was a hidden treasure, and wanted to be known' (see Annemarie Schimmel, *The Triumphal Sun: A Study of the Works of Jalāloddin Rumi*, London, East-West Publications, 1980, p. 225).

43

[T409; N355]
This *ghazal* provides a clear description of an extraordinary experience of mystical consciousness occasioned by a 'visitation' of the poet's Beloved. What is important in this is the step by step recounting of the poet's altered state experience, which indicates the purpose of this *ghazal* as a didactic poem explaining to novices the expectations of altered consciousness. See further Kenneth Avery, 'The Poet as Teacher: ʿAṭṭār and Personal Expression', *Sufi*, no. 51, 2001, pp.14-19.
v.7 Night or early dawn is usually the time for such experiences, being the hours of prayer and meditation (Cf. Shabistarī's encounter mentioned in his *Gulshan-i Rāz* [Ṣ. Muwaḥḥid(ed.), Tehran, Kitāb-khāna-yi Taḥūrī, 1371 a.h.s., lines 981ff]). '[D]runk and asleep' refers to a state of hypoarousal prepared by meditation and spiritual discipline, a state of deep awareness which blocks out the external world.
v.10 Cf. Rūmī: 'the body becomes all soul, every hair tip alive.' (Arberry, A.J., *Mystical Poems of Rūmī*, Chicago and London, University of Chicago Press, 1968, 143.7)
v.12 His soul 'had much to say' but his tongue was useless, since these 'words' were sublimely inexpressible. He had passed into a state beyond the possibility of speech, the state Rūmī constantly urges us to attain:

> 'I have closed the passage of the lips, and opened the secret way;
> I am free in one moment from the desire of speech.' (*DST* 39.12)

v.14 The experience of *fanā'* and *baqā'*, the passing away of mundane consciousness and remaining in the divine presence, alternating between dying and living, burning like the dawn candle.
v.19 'bathhouse' is a metaphor of the world.
v.20 Beating 'water in the mortar' suggests something futile, but the expression has sexual connotations: *hāwan* (mortar) also means 'vulva'.
v.23 The poet ends by suggesting that he has still only taken the first step in his journey of the soul; this outline of his extraordinary experience would argue otherwise, but perhaps he is expressing fellow-feeling with younger aspirants on the Path.

44

[T447; N403]
A *ghazal* of the *qalandarī* genre, showing scorn of hypocritical piety and asceticism, and commendation of the dissolute life of the antinomian Sufi 'lover'.

45

[T520; N468]
Passing beyond the distinctions between faith and infidelity, certainty and doubt, is a necessary step along the path of divine love. This *ghazal* attempts to sketch the world seen by the poet in a vision of the Beloved, occasioned by the suggestive rhyme 'I saw' (*dīdam*).
v.4 'Alexander's rampart' is a reference to Qur'ān 18.93-98, where Dhū 'l-Qarnayn (traditionally interpreted as Alexander the Great) generously built a protective rampart or barrier (*sadd*) to defend an unnamed group of people he met on his expeditions.
v.11 'Rakhsh', the horse of the celebrated Iranian hero Rustam, from Firdawsī's *Book of Kings*.
v.20 Cf. note on *ghazal* 17, v.9 above.

46

[T618; N557]
This *ghazal* explores the subject of Creation and the primordial covenant of God with yet to be created humankind, known as *Alast* (Qur. 7.172). God asked humankind whether they acknowledged Him as their Lord (*alastu bi-rabbikum*), to which the reply was 'Yes!'. The poetic interpretation of this Qur'ānic theme as the 'banquet' of *Alast*, and the first drunkenness deriving from its pre-eternal wine, became a central tenet of Sufi thought and poetry, evidenced by the most famous mystical poem in Arabic of Ibn al-Fāriḍ (See note on ghazal 6, v.17 above).
v.4 The quote in the first half verse is from Qur'ān 76.21, where God gives a drink of pure wine to the righteous in heaven.
v.5 The reference to the kneading of Adam's clay for forty days comes from a *ḥadīth* (sacred Tradition) to that effect, based on Qur'ān 38.71-2.
v.8 Perhaps a reference to the *ḥadīth* 'I am with those whose hearts are broken for my sake' (see Annemarie Schimmel, *The Triumphal Sun: A Study of the Works of Jalāloddin Rumi*, London, East-West Publications, 1980, pp. 278,323-4).

47

[T657; N596]
The opening question 'What's being in Love?' receives eloquent answer in this *ghazal*, using traditional themes and symbols, such as the moth, the Path, the bloodied heart, etc. There are some similarities with the sublime poem of Rūmī, *DST* 35 (see note on *ghazal* 17, v.9 above).

48

[T668; N606]
Another *ghazal* of the *qalandarī* or 'antinomian' genre where the poet expresses the infamy or disrepute of the genuine mystic's path, in contrast with the false attitudes and hypocrisy of outwardly respectable piety.

49

[T783; N713]
v.5 Wild rue was burned to ward off the 'evil eye'.

50

[T816; N747]
v.1 The divine essence is at the centre of the soul, and yet hidden from it like a treasure, recalling the *ḥadīth* (sacred Tradition) 'I was a hidden treasure and wanted to be known'.

BIBLIOGRAPHY

Abū Sa'īd b. Abī 'l-Khayr, *Sukhunān-i manẓūm*, Sa'īd Nafīsī (ed.), Tehran, Kitābkhāna-yi Sanā'ī, 1349 a.h.s.

Ibn Al-'Arabī, Muḥyi'ddīn, *The Tarjumān al-Ashwāq: A Collection of Mystical Odes*, trans. Reynold A. Nicholson (ed.), London, Theosophical Publishing House, 1978.

Arberry, A.J., *Arabic Poetry: A Primer for Students*, Cambridge, Cambridge University Press, 1965.

Arberry, A.J., *Classical Persian Literature*, London, George Allen & Unwin, 1958.

Arberry, A.J., *Discourses of Rūmī.*, Richmond, Curzon Press, 1993 repr.

Arberry, A.J., *Fifty Poems of Ḥāfiẓ*, Cambridge, Cambridge University Press, 1947; repr. 1977.

Arberry, A.J., *Immortal Rose: An Anthology of Persian Lyrics*, London, Luzac & Co, 1948.

Arberry, A.J., *Mystical Poems of Rūmī*, Chicago and London, University of Chicago Press, 1968.

Ashtiany, Julia, *et al* (eds.), *The Cambridge History of Arabic Literature: 'Abbasid Belles-Lettres*, Cambridge, Cambridge University Press, 1990.

'Aṭṭār, Farīd al-Dīn, *Asrār-nāma*, Sayyid Ṣ. Gawharīn (ed.), Tehran, Kitābfurūshī Zawwār, 1361 a.h.s.

'Aṭṭār, Farīd al-Dīn, *The Conference of the Birds*, trans. A. Darbandi and D. Davis. Harmondsworth, Penguin, 1984.

'Aṭṭār, Farīd al-Dīn, *Dīwān*, M. Darwīsh (ed.), Tehran, Intishārāt Jāwīdān, 1359 a.h.s.

'Aṭṭār, Farīd al-Dīn, *Dīwān*, Sa'īd Nafīsī (ed.), Tehran, Kitābkhāna-yi Sanā'ī, 1339 a.h.s.

'Aṭṭār, Farīd al-Dīn, *Dīwān*, Taqī Tafaḍḍulī (ed.), Tehran, Bungāh-i Tarjama u Nashri Kitāb, 1967.

'Aṭṭār, Farīd al-Dīn, *Ilahi-nāma*, H. Ritter (ed.), Istanbul, Maṭba'a ma'ārif, 1940.

'Aṭṭār, Farīd al-Dīn, *Manṭiq al-ṭayr*, M.J. Mashkūr (ed.), Tehran, Kitābfurūshī Tehran, 1353 a.h.s.

'Aṭṭār, Farīd al-Dīn, *Mukhtār-nāma*, Mahmud R.S. Kadkanī (ed.), Tehran, Sukhun, 1375 a.h.s.

'Aṭṭār, Farīd al-Dīn, *Muṣībat-nāma*, Nūrānī Wisāl (ed.), Tehran, Intishārāt Zawwār, 1338 a.h.s.

'Aṭṭār, Farīd al-Dīn, *Muslim Saints and Mystics*, trans. A.J. Arberry, London, Routledge & Kegan Paul, 1979.

'Aṭṭār, Farīd al-Dīn, *The Tadhkiratu 'l-awliyā*, R.A. Nicholson (ed.), 2 vols., London & Leiden, E.J. Brill; Luzac & Co, 1905-7.

Avery, Kenneth, 'The Poet as Teacher: 'Aṭṭār and Personal Expression', *Sufi*, no. 51, 2001, pp.14-19.

Avery, Kenneth, 'The Theme of the Sufi Master and the Tavern in the Lyric Poetry of 'Aṭṭār', *Sufi*, no. 48, 2000/01, pp.8-13.

'Awfī, Muḥammad, *Lubābu 'l-albāb*, E.G. Browne and M.M. Qazwīnī (eds.), Tehran, Kitābfurūshī Fakhr-Rāzī, 1361 a.h.s. repr.

Bausani, Alessandro, 'The Development of Form in Persian Lyrics: A Way to the Better Understanding of the Structure of Western Poetry', *East and West*, no. 9, 1958, pp.145-153.

Bausani, Alessandro, 'Religion in the Saljuq Period', in J.A. Boyle (ed.), *The Cambridge History of Iran*, vol. 5, Cambridge, Cambridge University Press, 1968, pp.283-302.

Bausani, Alessandro and Blachère, R., 'Ghazal' in *Encyclopaedia of Islam*, vol. II, Leiden, E.J. Brill, 1960-, pp.1028-1036.

Benjamin, Walter, *Illuminations*, trans. H. Zohn, London, Fontana, 1992.

Blois, François de, *Persian Literature: A Biobibliographical Survey, begun by the late C.A. Storey*, vol. 1, part 2, London, The Royal Asiatic Society of Great Britain and Ireland, 1994.

Bosworth, C.E., 'The Political and Dynastic History of the Iranian World (A.D. 1000-1217)' in J.A. Boyle (ed.), *The Cambridge History of Iran*, vol. 5, Cambridge, Cambridge University Press, 1968, pp.1-202.

Boyle, J.A. (ed.), *The Cambridge History of Iran*, vol. 5, Cambridge, Cambridge University Press, 1968.

Boyle, J.A., *The Ilāhīnama or Book of God of Farīd al-Dīn 'Aṭṭār*, Manchester, Manchester University Press, 1976.

Bruijn, J.T.P. de, 'Comparative Notes on Sana'i and 'Aṭṭār', *Sufi*, no. 16, 1992-3, pp.13-19; repr. in Leonard Lewisohn (ed.), *Classical Persian Sufism: From its Origins to Rumi*, London, Khaniqahi Nimatullahi Publications, 1993, pp.361-379.

Bruijn, J.T.P. de, *Of Piety and Poetry: The Interaction of Religion and Literature in the Life and Works of Ḥakīm Sanā'ī of Ghazna*, Leiden, E.J. Brill, 1983.

Bruijn, J.T.P. de, *Persian Sufi Poetry: An Introduction to the Mystical use of Classical Persian Poems*, Richmond, Curzon Press, 1997.

Bruijn, J.T.P. de, 'The Preaching Poet: Three Homiletic Poems by Farīd al-Dīn 'Aṭṭār', *Edebiyāt*, no. 9, 1998, pp.85-100.

Bruijn, J.T.P. de, 'The Qalandariyyāt in Persian Mystical Poetry, from Sanā'ī Onwards' in Leonard Lewisohn (ed.), *The Legacy of Mediaeval Persian Sufism*, London, Khaniqahi Nimatullahi Publications, 1992, pp.75-86.

Bruijn, J.T.P. de, 'Sanā'ī', in *Encyclopaedia of Islam*, vol. IX, Leiden, E.J. Brill, 1960-, pp.3-5.

Bruijn, J.T.P. de, 'Sanā'ī and the Rise of Persian Mystical Poetry', *La signification du Bas Moyen age dans l'histoire et la culture du monde musulman: Actes du 8me Congrès de l'Union européenne des arabisants et islamisants*, Aix-en-Provence, 1978, pp.35-43.

Bulliet, Richard W., *The Patricians of Nishapur: A Study in Medieval Islamic Social History*, Cambridge (Mass.), Harvard University Press, 1972.

Bürgel, J.C., 'Love, Lust and Longing: Eroticism in Early Islam as Reflected in Literary Sources' in A.L. Sayyid-Marsot (ed.), *Society and the Sexes in Medieval Islam*, Malibu, Undena, 1979, pp.81-117.

Burton, John, 'Quranic Exegesis', in M.J.L. Young et al (eds.), *The Cambridge History of Arabic Literature: Religion, Learning and Science in the 'Abbasid Period*, Cambridge, Cambridge University Press, 1990, pp.40-55.

Chelkowski, P.J. (ed.), *The Scholar and the Saint*, New York, New York University Press, 1975.

Correale, Daniela Meneghini and Zanolla, Valentina, *'Aṭṭār Concordance and Lexical Repertories of 1000 lines*, Venice, Università degli Studi di Venezia, 1993.

Dabashi, Hamid, 'Historical Conditions of Persian Sufism during the Seljuk Period', in Leonard Lewisohn (ed.), *Classical Persian Sufism: From its Origins to Rumi*, London, Khaniqahi Nimatullahi Publications, 1993, pp.137-174.

Dawlatshāh Samarqandī, *Tadhkirat al-shu'arā'*, M. Ramḍānī (ed.), Tehran, Khāwar, 1344 a.h.s.

Derrida, Jacques, *Of Grammatology*, trans. G.C. Spivak, Baltimore, Johns Hopkins University Press, 1976.

Encyclopaedia Iranica, E. Yarshater (ed.), London, New York, Routledge & Kegan Paul, 1989-.

Encyclopaedia of Islam, new ed., Leiden, E.J. Brill, 1960-.

Ernst, Carl W., *Rūzbihān Baqlī: Mysticism and the Rhetoric of Sainthood in Persian Sufism*, Richmond, Curzon Press, 1996.

Este'lami, M., 'The Study of Narratives and Realities in 'Aṭṭār's Work', *Sufi*, no. 59, 2003, pp.31-35.

Foucault, Michel, *The History of Sexuality: 1 – The Will to Knowledge*, trans. R. Hurley, London, Penguin, 1990.

Frye, R.N. (ed.), *The Cambridge History of Iran*, vol. 4, Cambridge, Cambridge University Press, 1975.

Frye, R.N., *The Golden Age of Persia: The Arabs in the East*, London, Weidenfeld & Nicolson, 1975.

Furūzānfar, Badī' al-Zamān, *Sharḥ-i aḥwāl wa naqd wa taḥlīl-i āthār-i Shaykh Farīd al-Dīn Muḥammad 'Aṭṭār*, Tehran, Kitābfurūshī Dih-khudā, 1353 a.h.s.

Glünz, Michael, and Bürgel, J. Christoph (eds.), *Intoxication Earthly and Heavenly: Seven Studies on the Poet Hafiz of Shiraz*, Bern, Peter Lang, 1991.

Glünz, Michael, 'The Poet's Heart: A Polyfunctional Object in the Poetic System of the Ghazal', in Glünz, Michael, and Bürgel, J. Christoph (eds.), *Intoxication Earthly and Heavenly: Seven Studies on the Poet Hafiz of Shiraz*, Bern, Peter Lang, 1991, pp.53-68.

Graham, Terry, 'Abū Sa'īd ibn Abī 'l-Khayr and the School of Khurāsān', in Leonard Lewisohn (ed.), *Classical Persian Sufism: From its Origins to Rumi*, London, Khaniqahi Nimatullahi Publications, 1993, pp.83-135.

Ḥāfiẓ Shīrāzī, *Dīwān*, M. Qazwīnī and Q. Ghanī (eds.), Tehran, Chāpkhāna-yi Majlis, 1320 a.h.s.

Hamid, Farooq, 'Storytelling Techniques in the Masnavī-yi Ma'navī of Mowlana Jalal al-Din Rumi: Wayward Narrative or Logical Progression?', *Iranian Studies*, vol. 32, no. 1, 1999, pp.27-49.

Hamori, A., 'Ascetic Poetry (Zuhdiyyāt)', in *The Cambridge History of Arabic Literature: 'Abbasid Belles-Lettres*, Julia Ashtiany et al (eds.), Cambridge, Cambridge University Press, 1990, pp.265-274.

Hamori, A., 'Love Poetry (Ghazal)', in *The Cambridge History of Arabic Literature: 'Abbasid Belles-Lettres*, Julia Ashtiany et al (eds.), Cambridge, Cambridge University Press, 1990, pp.202-218.

Harb, F., 'Wine Poetry (Khamriyyāt)', in *The Cambridge History of Arabic Literature: 'Abbasid Belles-Lettres*, Julia Ashtiany et al (eds.), Cambridge, Cambridge University Press, 1990, pp.219-234.

Hillmann, Michael C., *Unity in the Ghazals of Hafez*, Minneapolis, Bibliotheca Islamica, 1976.

The Holy Quran: Text, Translation and Commentary, trans. Abdullah Yusuf Ali, Lahore, Ashraf, 1938; repr. 1977.

Honigmann, E. (and Bosworth, C.E.), 'Nīshāpūr', in *Encyclopaedia of Islam*, vol. VIII, Leiden, E.J. Brill, 1960-, pp.62-64.

Jāmī, 'Abd al-Raḥman b. Aḥmad, *Nafaḥāt al-uns min ḥaḍarāt al-quds*, M. Tawḥīdī Pūr (ed.), Tehran, 'Ilmī, 1375 a.h.s.

Kennedy, Philip F., *The Wine Song in Classical Arabic Poetry: Abū Nuwās and the Literary Tradition*, Oxford, Clarendon Press, 1997.

Keshavarz, Fatemeh, *Reading Mystical Lyric: The Case of Jalal al-Din Rumi*, Columbia S.C., University of South Carolina Press, 1998.

Khairallah, As'ad E., *Love, Madness and Poetry: An Interpretation of the Mağnūn Legend*, Beirut, Franz Steiner Verlag, 1980.

Ibn Khalaf Tabrīzī, Muḥammad Ḥusayn, *Burhān-i Qāṭi'*, M. Mu'īn (ed.), Tehran, Amīr Kabīr, 1982.

Knysh, Alexander, *Islamic Mysticism: A Short History*, Leiden, Boston, Köln, Brill, 2000.

The Koran Interpreted, trans. A.J. Arberry, Oxford, Oxford University Press, 1964; repr. 1991.

Lambton, Ann K.S., *Continuity and Change in Medieval Persia: Aspects of Administrative, Economic and Social History, 11th-14th Century*, Albany (N.Y.), The Persian Heritage Foundation, 1988.

Lambton, Ann K.S., 'The Internal Structure of the Saljuq Empire', *The Cambridge History of Iran*, vol. 5, J.A. Boyle (ed.), Cambridge, Cambridge University Press, 1968, pp.203-282.

Lambton, Ann K.S., *Persian Grammar*, Cambridge, Cambridge University Press, 1953; repr. 1976.

Lazard, G., *Dictionnaire persan-français*, Leiden, E.J. Brill, 1990.

Lazard, G., 'The Rise of the New Persian Language', in *The Cambridge History of Iran*, vol. 4, R.N. Frye (ed.), Cambridge, Cambridge University Press, 1975, pp.595-632.

Levy, Reuben (trans.), *The Epic of the Kings: Shah-Nama the national epic of Persia by Ferdowsi*, London, Henley and Boston, Routledge & Kegan Paul, 1967.

Lewisohn, Leonard, *Beyond Faith and Infidelity: The Sufi Poetry and Teachings of Maḥmūd Shabistarī*, Richmond, Curzon Press, 1995.

Lewisohn, Leonard (ed.), *Classical Persian Sufism: From its Origins to Rumi*, London, Khaniqahi Nimatullahi Publications, 1993.

Lewisohn, Leonard (ed.), *The Legacy of Medieval Persian Sufism*, London, Khaniqahi Nimatullahi Publications, 1992.

Lewisohn, Leonard, 'Overview: Iranian Islam and Persianate Sufism', in *The Legacy of Medieval Persian Sufism*, London, Khaniqahi Nimatullahi Publications, 1992, pp.11-43.

Lings, M., 'Mystical Poetry', in *The Cambridge History of Arabic Literature: 'Abbasid Belles-Lettres*, Julia Ashtiany et al (eds.), Cambridge, Cambridge University Press, 1990, pp.235-264.

Losensky, Paul E., 'Linguistic and Rhetorical Aspects of the Signature Verse (Takhalluṣ) in the Persian Ghazal', *Edebiyāt*, no. 8, 1998, pp.239-271.

Malamud, Margaret, 'Sufi Organizations and Structures of Authority in Medieval Nishapur', *International Journal of Middle East Studies*, no. 26, 1994, pp.427-442.

Meisami, Julie Scott, 'Allegorical Gardens in the Persian Poetic Tradition: Nezami, Rumi, Hafez', *International Journal of Middle East Studies*, no. 17, 1985, pp.229-260.

Meisami, Julie Scott, 'The Ghazal as Fiction: Implied Speakers and Implied Audience in Hafiz's Ghazals', in Glünz, Michael, and Bürgel, J. Christoph (eds.), *Intoxication Earthly and Heavenly: Seven Studies on the Poet Hafiz of Shiraz*, Bern, Peter Lang, 1991, pp.89-103.

Meisami, Julie Scott, *Medieval Persian Court Poetry*, Princeton, Princeton University Press, 1987.

Meisami, Julie Scott, *Structure and Meaning in Medieval Arabic and Persian Poetry: Orient Pearls*, London & New York, RoutledgeCurzon, 2003.

Moayyad, Heshmat, 'Lyric Poetry', in E. Yarshater (ed.), *Persian Literature*, Albany (N.Y.), Persian Heritage Foundation, 1988, pp.120-146.

Mukhtasar Tafsīr Ibn Kathīr, Beirut, Dār al-Maʿrifa, 1995.

Nicholson, R.A. (ed. and trans.), *The Mathnawī of Jalālu'ddīn Rūmī*, London, E.J.W. Gibb Memorial Trust; Luzac & Co, 1925-40.

Nicholson, R.A., *Selected Poems from the Dīvāni Shamsi Tabrīz*, Cambridge, Cambridge University Press, 1898; repr.1977.

Nicholson, R.A., *Studies in Islamic Mysticism*, Cambridge, Cambridge University Press, 1921; repr. 1980.

Niẓāmī Ganjawī, *Dīwān*, Saʿīd Nafīsī (ed.), Tehran, Furūghī, 1380 a.h.s.

Nwyia, Paul, *Exégèse coranique et langage mystique*, Beirut, Dar el-Machreq sarl, 1991.

Nwyia, Paul, 'Le Tafsīr mystique attribué à Ǧaʿfar Ṣādiq', *Mélanges de l'Université Saint-Joseph*, vol. XLIII, no. 4, 1968, pp.179-230.

Platts, John T., and Ranking, George S.A., *A Grammar of the Persian Language*, Oxford, Clarendon Press, 1911.

Pritchett, Frances W., 'Orient Pearls Unstrung: The Quest for Unity in the Ghazal' in *Edebiyāt*, no. 4, 1993, pp.119-135.

Rehder, Robert M., 'The Style of Jalāl al-Dīn Rūmī', in Chelkowski, P.J. (ed.), *The Scholar and the Saint*, New York, New York University Press, 1975, pp.275-285.

Reinert, Benedikt, "Aṭṭār', in *Encyclopaedia Iranica*, E. Yarshater (ed.), vol. III, London, New York, Routledge & Kegan Paul, 1989, pp.20-25.

Ritter, Hellmut, "Aṭṭār', in *Encyclopaedia of Islam*, vol. I, new ed., Leiden, E.J. Brill, 1960-, pp.752-755.

Ritter, Hellmut, *Das Meer der Seele: Mensch, Welt und Gott in den Geschichten des Farīduddīn 'Aṭṭār*, Leiden, E.J. Brill, 1978.

Ritter, Hellmut, 'Philologika XV Farīduddīn 'Aṭṭār III.7. Der Dīwān', *Oriens*, no. 12, 1959, pp.1-88.

Rypka, Jan, *History of Iranian Literature*, Dordrecht, D. Reidel, 1968.

Rypka, Jan, 'Poets and Prose Writers of the Late Saljuq and Mongol Periods', in *The Cambridge History of Iran*, vol. 5, J.A. Boyle (ed.), Cambridge, Cambridge University Press, 1968, pp.550-625.

Sanāʾī Ghaznawī, Ḥakīm, *Dīwān*, M. Raḍawī (ed.), Tehran, Kitābkhāna-yi Sanāʾī, 1355 a.h.s.

Savory, R.M. (ed.), *Introduction to Islamic Civilization*, Cambridge, Cambridge University Press, 1976.

Al-Sayyid-Marsot, Afaf Lutfi (ed.), *Society and the Sexes in Medieval Islam*, Malibu, Undena, 1979.

Schimmel, Annemarie, *As Through a Veil: Mystical Poetry in Islam*, New York, Columbia University Press, 1982.

Schimmel, Annemarie, *Calligraphy and Islamic Culture*, New York & London, New York University Press, 1984.

Schimmel, Annemarie, 'Eros—Heavenly and not so Heavenly—in Sufi Literature and Life', in A.L. Sayyid-Marsot (ed.), *Society and the Sexes in Medieval Islam*, Malibu, Undena, 1979, pp.119-141.

Schimmel, Annemarie, *I am Wind, You are Fire: The Life and Work of Rumi,* Boston, Shambhala, 1996.

Schimmel, Annemarie, *Mystical Dimensions of Islam*, Chapel Hill, University of North Carolina Press, 1975.

Schimmel, Annemarie, *Stern und Blume: Die Bilderwelt der persischen Poesie,* Wiesbaden, Harrassowitz, 1984.

Schimmel, Annemarie, *The Triumphal Sun: A Study of the Works of Jalāloddin Rumi*, London & The Hague, East-West Publications, 1980.

Schimmel, Annemarie, 'Turk and Hindu: A Literary Symbol', *Acta Iranica*, no. 3, 1974, pp.243-248.

Sells, Michael A., *Mystical Languages of Unsaying*, Chicago & London, University of Chicago Press, 1994.

Shabistarī, Shaykh Maḥmūd, *Majmū'a-i āthār*, Ṣ. Muwaḥḥid (ed.), Tehran, Kitābkhāna-yi Taḥūrī, 1371 a.h.s.

Shajī'ī, Pūrān, *Jihān-bīnī-yi 'Aṭṭār*, Tehran, Ḥaydarī, 1373 a.h.s.

The Shorter Encyclopaedia of Islam, H.A.R. Gibb and J.H. Kramers (eds.), Leiden, E.J. Brill, 1953; repr.1974.

Skalmowski, W., 'The Meaning of the Persian Ghazal', *Orientalia Lovaniensia Periodica,* no. 18, 1987, pp.141-162.

Skalmowski, W., 'Notes on the Ghazals of Sa'di and Hafiz', *Orientalia Lovaniensia Periodica*, no. 10, 1979, pp.255-273.

Steingass, F., *Persian-English Dictionary*, London, Routledge & Kegan Paul, 1892; 1977.

Stetkevych, Suzanne Pinckney, 'Intoxication and Immortality: Wine and Associated Imagery in al-Ma'arrī's Garden', in Wright, J.W.(jr), and Rowson, Everett K. (eds.), *Homoeroticism in Classical Arabic Literature*, New York, Columbia University Press, 1997, pp.210-232.

Stetkevych, Suzanne Pinckney (ed.), *Reorientations / Arabic and Persian Poetry*, Bloomington & Indianapolis, Indiana University Press, 1994.

Tafsīr al-Imāmayn al-Jalālayn, Beirut, Dār al-Kutub al-ʿIlmīya, no date.

Trimingham, J. Spencer, *The Sufi Orders in Islam*, Oxford, Clarendon Press, 1971.

Valiuddin, Mir, *Contemplative Disciplines in Sufism*, London & The Hague, East-West Publications, 1980.

Vullers, I.A., *Lexicon Persico-Latinum etymologicum*, Graz, Akademische Druck-u. Verlagsanstalt, 1855-64; repr. 1962.

Wickens, G.M., 'The Frozen Periphery of Allusion in Classical Persian Literature' in *Literature East and West*, vol. 18, nos. 2-4, 1974, pp.171-190.

Wickens, G.M., 'Persian Literature: an Affirmation of Identity', in Savory, R.M. (ed.), *Introduction to Islamic Civilization*, Cambridge, Cambridge University Press, 1976, pp.71-78.

Wright, J.W.(jr), and Rowson, Everett K. (eds.), *Homoeroticism in Classical Arabic Literature*, New York, Columbia University Press, 1997.

Yarshater, E. (ed.), *Persian Literature*, Albany (N.Y.), Persian Heritage Foundation, 1988.

Yarshater, E., 'Some Common Characteristics of Persian Poetry and Art', *Studia Islamica*, no. 16, 1962, pp.61-71.

Yarshater, E., 'The Theme of Wine-drinking and the Concept of the Beloved in Early Persian Poetry', *Studia Islamica*, no. 13, 1960, pp.43-53.

Yazici, Tahsin, 'Ḳalandar' and 'Ḳalandariyya', in *Encyclopaedia of Islam*, vol. IV, new ed., Leiden, E.J. Brill, 1960-, pp.472-474.

Young, M.J.L., *et al* (eds.), *The Cambridge History of Arabic Literature: Religion, Learning and Science in the 'Abbasid Period*, Cambridge, Cambridge University Press, 1990.

CPSIA information can be obtained at www.ICGtesting.com
Printed in the USA
LVOW06s0223270715

447749LV00001B/66/P

9 780980 305210